CHINESE MEDICINE FROM THE CLASSICS
A BEGINNER'S GUIDE

CHINESE MEDICINE FROM THE CLASSICS

Claude Larre:
The Way of Heaven: Suwen chapters 1 and 2

Claude Larre and Elisabeth Rochat de la Vallée:
The Secret Treatise of the Spiritual Orchid: Suwen chapter 8
The Heart in Lingshu chapter 8
The Lung
The Kidneys
The Spleen and Stomach
Heart Master, Triple Heater
The Liver
Essence, Spirit, Blood and Qi
The Seven Emotions
The Eight Extraordinary Meridians
The Extraordinary Fu

Elisabeth Rochat de la Vallée:
A Study of Qi
Yin Yang in Classical Texts
The Essential Woman
Pregnancy and Gestation
Wu Xing: The Five Elements
The Rhythm at the Heart of the World: Suwen chapter 5
The Double Aspect of the Heart
Aspects of Spirit

Group translation:
Jing Shen: Huainanzi chapter 7

MONKEY PRESS

CHINESE MEDICINE FROM THE CLASSICS
A BEGINNER'S GUIDE
Sandra Hill

MONKEY PRESS
Monkey Press is named after the Monkey King in The Journey to the West, the 16th century novel by Wu Chengen. Monkey blends skill, initiative and wisdom with the spirit of freedom, irreverence and a touch of mischief.

CHINESE MEDICINE FROM THE CLASSICS:
A BEGINNER'S GUIDE
Sandra Hill

Published by
Monkey Press
www.monkeypress.net
info@monkeypress.net

© Monkey Press 2014

All rights reserved. No part of this book may be reproduced in any form without written permission from the publisher.

ISBN 978 1 872468 15 0

Cover image: A section of the Mawangdui funeral banner; adapted from a photograph courtesy of Graham Challifour
Calligraphy: Qu Lei Lei
Printed and bound in the UK by Short Run Press

CONTENTS

Foreword	vii
Preface	ix
PHILOSOPHICAL ROOTS	1
Dao	2
Yin yang	6
Wu xing: five elements/phases	13
The three treasures:	21
Shen	22
Jing	24
Qi	25
THE FIVE ZANG	30
Kidneys	32
Liver	43
Heart	54
Spleen	65
Lung	75
THE SIX FU	84
Stomach	86
Gallbladder	89
Small intestine	92
Large intestine	95
Bladder	98
TRIPLE HEATER	102
THE EXTRAORDINARY FU	112

THE EMOTIONS	121
Anger	125
Joy and elation	129
Fear	133
Thinking	137
Sadness and Oppression	140
Fright	143
THE FIVE ASPECTS OF SPIRIT	145
Shen	149
Hun	150
Po	153
Yi	156
Zhi	159
THE MERIDIAN NETWORK	162
Mai	164
Jing	166
Luo	170
Jing bie	171
Jing jin	171
THE EXTRAORDINARY MERIDIANS	174
Du mai	176
Ren mai	179
Chong mai	182
Dai mai	186
Yin and yang qiao mai	190
Yin and yang wei mai	193
Afterword	201
Index	205
Glossary	214
Text References	218

FOREWORD

In order to practice Chinese medicine in the West it is necessary to master the fundamentals on which the practice is based. But it is always challenging to enter into a way of thinking, a language, a civilization that is not ours by birth. Chinese medicine was developed a very long time ago, in a distant place, with a language and a vision of life we are not at all familiar with, but its future development belongs not only to China and the Chinese. Because we share the experience of being human, living within a human body, Chinese medicine can be used and practiced by non-Chinese people, and it can continue to evolve throughout the world. But a true understanding of its roots, of its vision of life, health, disorder and disease, is absolutely necessary in order to build a firm foundation both for its practice and for its development in the future.

Sandra Hill has been aware of the importance of this for a long time. From her initial studies in Japan, she went on to nourish her practice by engaging with the classical texts and those who work directly with them. She finally took on the difficult task of editing seminars on classical Chinese medicine which interpreted and elucidated these texts.

The Chinese medical texts have a long history. At the time of the Warring States (453 – 221 BCE) and the Early Han (206 BCE – 8 AD), reflections were beginning to appear on the nature of what it means to be human – on psychology and on the art of attaining longevity or 'nurturing life' (*yang sheng*). Descriptions of the human body began to appear which reflected what was being observed on earth and in the cosmos. The same *qi* animate both human beings and nature. This understanding of life was gradually organized in general patterns, such as the theory of *yin yang* and five elements (*yin yang wu xing*), and theoretical medical approaches emerged from all these considerations.

The oldest texts on medicine available to us now are manuscripts discovered in tombs dating from the end of the 3rd century and the middle of the 2nd century BCE. From the time of the Han onwards (221 BCE – 220 AD), a more coherent presentation was elaborated, based on a doctrine which bears the mark of the social and political organization of the time. These texts, partly re-written and edited in later times, were brought together in various compilations.

Among the most important, is the Huangdi Neijing or Inner Classic of the Yellow Emperor. Traditionally, it consists of the Simple Questions (Suwen) and the Spiritual Pivot (Lingshu). Their final compilation was relatively late (8th century for the Suwen and 12th century for the Lingshu), but they contain re-drafts from the time of the Warring States to the end of the Han, with alterations and additions along the way – possibly up to the beginning of the Tang dynasty (618 – 907). There have been many commentaries and studies on these texts.

The Monkey Press publications are based on these two texts which form the Inner Classic of the Yellow Emperor. The particular extracts were selected to give the reader general, but precise and useful, information on what is essential to the understanding of Chinese medicine. They are explained within the context of their particular civilization and time, thus helping to deepen understanding, root the practice and avoid misinterpretation. But these books are an immersion in the Chinese world which can overwhelm some beginners.

Sandra Hill has achieved an admirable work with this guide, which is a clear and intelligent introduction to Chinese medicine as it is expressed in these classical texts. It provides access for further reading and deeper study. I am personally immensely grateful to her.

Elisabeth Rochat de la Vallée, Paris 2014

PREFACE

Monkey Press was created in order to bring the teaching of the classical Chinese scholars Claude Larre sj. and Elisabeth Rochat de la Vallée to an English speaking audience. The series began with a transcription of a seminar given on the text of Neijing Suwen chapter 8, The Secret Treatise of the Spiritual Orchid, a seminal text which presents the functions of the twelve internal organs as if they were officials within the emperor's court. The photocopied notes proved to be in demand, a more sophisticated approach was called for, and gradually Monkey Press was established.

At the time of the early seminars, the Chinese medical community in the West was experiencing an ideological division between the so-called five element and eight conditions systems, and for many of us who felt alienated by this spurious separation, access to the Chinese classical texts broke through any simplistic ideas of division and segregation, confirming that this is not an either/or medicine, but a medicine of vast scope and interpretation. Attempts to make a straightforward system of classification – whether according to five element correspondence or TCM principles, became irrelevant in the light of this knowledge. The medicine of the Huangdi Neijing is certainly eclectic and may at times seem contradictory, but its fundamental philosophy is consistent and sound, and provides a firm foundation for any kind of practice.

The present book is an attempt to introduce both the Monkey Press series and the text of the Huangdi Neijing, and is written in answer to requests by students for an approachable introduction to the subject. It is completely dependent on the scholarship of Claude and Elisabeth, with whom I have studied for close to 30 years. My own interest in Chinese medicine grew from a fascination with oriental philosophy, which took me to Japan in the early 1970s. I studied both martial arts and bodywork, before embarking on an intensive training with a shinto priest who also practiced acupuncture. This was at a time before the introduction of TCM into Japan, and my initial training in Chinese medicine was based on palpation and the development of sensitivity towards *qi*. Traditionally, acupuncture was a career favoured by the blind, and the development of both palpation techniques and specific types of subtle needling grew out of this.

It was soon after the completion of my acupuncture training at the International College of Oriental Medicine in the UK that Claude Larre spoke at a conference on Chinese medicine organized by the Traditional Acupuncture Society. During a panel discussion on the nature of *qi*, Father Larre suggested that while it may be helpful to give *qi* 35 names, above all it is something to be felt, to be lived, to be breathed – and that in all our academic study and research, this must never be forgotten.

And this was the feeling that he brought to the series of lectures established in London by the International Register for Oriental Medicine the following year. A kind of playfulness, an immediacy, which meant that the ideas were embodied and always made practical. The study of these classical texts was not simply for mental stimulation, or even spiritual philandering, as some suggested, but an attempt to understand the way in which the ancient Chinese saw the world, how they applied their observations in a clear and practical way in order to live most efficiently and effectively on earth, within a physical body. The texts examined the ways in which that worked (physiology) and the ways in which it might go wrong (pathology) – observing that the cause of deviation generally resides in human behaviour. The text of the Neijing therefore gives advice on the best way to behave, as well as the best way to guide the *qi* back to an alignment with the natural order.

The Monkey Press books aimed to extend the experience of those early seminars to the reader, and the first twelve books retained the conversational style of the lectures, with Claude bringing his vast knowledge of Chinese philosophy and culture, Elisabeth her in-depth understanding of the medical texts. With Claude's death in 2001, aged an auspicious 81 years, Elisabeth continued the teaching, and the transcripts moved into a new format. 17 books have now been transcribed and edited from lectures, three have been translated from the French, and *Jing Shen* (a translation of Huainanzi chapter 7) is a collaboration of the translation group that worked with Father Larre and Elisabeth over some 25 years. The texts of the Monkey Press series are referenced and footnoted throughout this book; all translations from the Chinese are by Claude and Elisabeth unless otherwise stated. In the few instances where the translation is not taken from a published text, it has been extracted from their seminar handouts.

In this present title, as with all the Monkey Press books, Chinese characters are used throughout the text, both to differentiate similar sounding terms, and to aid understanding. In classical Chinese, the etymology of characters can be helpful in deciphering meaning, and references are made to Wieger's Chinese Characters, which is based on the 2nd century CE dictionary, the Shuowen Jiezi. In analyzing a character, it may be divided into its constituent parts, often referred to as the radical or root, which places the character in a particular family or grouping, and its phonetic, which gives the sound as well as further refining the meaning. A glossary of the most commonly used Chinese terms is included after the index.

After some 30 years of study with Claude and Elisabeth, I have become increasingly aware that in order to translate classical Chinese texts, it is necessary to immerse oneself in the language, tradition and culture of that particular time. Until the recent publications of Paul Unschuld, there have been no reliable English translations of the Neijing, and Claude and Elisabeth remain amongst a very small group of scholars who may be considered equal to the task. Classical Chinese is by its nature ambiguous; the language is often poetic, and there is much play on words. Each character can convey a wealth of allusion in both its sound and structure, which allows for a vagueness and subtlety and often a deliberate lack of clarity, which cannot be conveyed in a word for word translation.

When reading a classical Chinese text in translation, it is therefore advisable to compare various translations in order to obtain a fuller picture; any translation is bound to reflect personal preference! By drawing only on Father Larre and Elisabeth's translations of the text, I am aware that I may be open to criticism, but academic scholarship and literary comparison is not the intention here. Their work is, above all, that of explanation and commentary; the translation only a starting point for elaboration and consideration. This book is primarily an introduction to the Monkey Press series, Chinese Medicine from the Classics, and as such, remains a tribute to their work.

I am therefore indebted to the dedication of Claude Larre and Elisabeth Rochat de la Vallée to the transmission of the Chinese classical texts. I have liberally used their scholarship, but I am ultimately responsible for the accuracy of this book. Any mistakes are mine. Peter Firebrace initiated both the seminar series and their transcription. His was the original inspiration for the establishment of Monkey Press. Caroline Root brought her publishing experience and editorial skills to the project to make it flourish, and continued to do so for many years. From the early days, Qu Lei Lei provided calligraphy for the books, and his work is gratefully used here to illustrate certain key terms. Mary Parsons, Anna Kiff, Justyna Gorska, Julia Smith and Nora Franglen kindly read through various drafts of this text and gave both encouragement and advice. Michelle Bromley has been indispensable in proofing both this and other recent Monkey publications. And finally, I would like to thank Julian Barnard and Healing Herbs for their generous support and encouragement.

Sandra Hill, London 2014

PHILOSOPHICAL ROOTS

During the 2nd century BCE, the first steps were taken to collate the medical knowledge of China and a compilation of this knowledge was written down in the form of the Yellow Emperor's Inner Classic (Huangdi Neijing). This was the Early Han dynasty, a time when previously feudal states were united under one emperor, and a common written language was used for the first time throughout the land. Scholars in various provinces were busy compiling texts from sources which included the great philosophical treatises of Daoism and Confucianism, as well as popular cosmology and shamanism. The text of the Neijing reflects the philosophical thinking of the time and constantly refers to the way in which human beings live by the intermingling of the influences of heaven (*tian* 天) and earth (*di* 地), endowed with a 'true nature' (*xing* 性) and the possibility of realizing an individual purpose or 'destiny' (*ming* 命).

According to the classical philosophical texts, the fulfilment of 'destiny' or of one's 'natural life-span' was to be achieved by following the *dao* (道) – though the best way to do that might differ amongst Daoists, Confucianists and shamans. Shamanism may suggest intercession through the spirits of the ancestors with spells and incantations, Confucianism appropriate behaviour and social order, and Daoism to follow what is 'naturally so'.

What is 'naturally so' (*zi ran* 自然) is a key concept within the early daoist texts, which present a world view of constant change and transformation, of the spontaneous emergence of life and its subsequent dissolution. An understanding of what is 'naturally so' is achieved by the close observation of nature – of how things come into being and how they behave. Elements of the natural world may be seen as archetypes of certain types and modes of being – their interactions symbolizing the way in which things change and transform.

The ability to change according to circumstance, but to maintain integrity of pattern and shape, is a primary definition of life. Life is that which constantly changes and transforms (*bian hua* 變 化), the 'changeless' is that from which life emerges and to which it returns. The *dao* could be said to be the way this all works – the inherent and natural order of life – which can be observed and followed, but which remains ultimately a mystery. The first chapter of the Daodejing tells us that 'the *dao* which we can speak of is not the eternal *dao*'[1], suggesting that as soon as we attempt to name and classify, to measure and probe these subtle mechanisms of life, we lose sight of them, they become something else under our gaze. The *dao* is the movement of life itself, bringing things into being, holding and sustaining them.

DAO 道

Chapter 42 of the Daodejing gives a concise description of the way in which life spontaneously arises; there is no external intelligence imposing order, but an implicit order emerging from life itself:

---

1 Laozi, Daodejing 道 德 經, The Way and its Virtue

'*Dao* gives rise to one
one gives rise to two
two gives rise to three
three gives rise to the ten thousand beings'

This is not a description of a creation event which happened in the past, but of a continual process of coming into being, changing and transforming and dissolving back into some kind of original chaos or unknowable mystery. Here the *dao* is before the one, before the state of unity which must then divide in order to bring about movement and change. The two remain, holding each other in a static balance until the emergence of three, which provides the dynamism to produce all life, symbolized by the ten thousand things or beings. The use of numbers to explain the constant unfolding and maintaining of life is seen throughout the scholarship of the time and plays an important part in the classical medical texts.

The opening lines of Huainanzi chapter 1, a philosophical daoist text contemporary with the Neijing, describes the universality of *dao*:

'As for *dao*:
It shelters heaven and supports the earth
extends beyond the four directions
opens to the eight extremities
high beyond reach
deep beyond reckoning
it envelops heaven and earth
and gives rise to the formless'[2]

---

[2] For a full translation of Huainanzi chapter 1 see Yuan Dao, Tracing the Dao to its Source, D.C. Lao, Roger Ames.

The *dao* supports and maintains all life, extending beyond the four directions and the eight extremities, the eight points of the compass which represent all conceivable space. It envelopes heaven and earth – in a way that suggests holding in a nurturing embrace (*bao* 包) – and gives rise to that which has no form. A key theme of the Huainanzi is this continual emergence and dissolution of life from a state of formlessness into form and returning back again to the formless. The *dao* gives rise to the formless, embracing everything from the largest possible expression of life to the smallest and most subtle; it both contains all things, and provides their source.

The formless, a state before physical manifestation, holds the patterns of life, as we see in the opening lines of Huainanzi chapter 7:

> 'In ancient times, when heaven and earth did not yet exist, there was only image (*xiang* 象) without form (*xing* 形)'.[3]

Before form comes into being, before matter coalesces into shape, there is an 'image' – an information patterning – which holds the potential for its manifestation. Structure is determined by this information pattern, just as a seed holds the potential for development, growth and adaptation. 'Information' is used here and in many places throughout the text to imply the way in which things come into being and take form. The Chinese *xiang* suggests this idea of a formative principle which guides the various ways in which matter takes shape, an image or pattern which must exist before form. And it is at this place, between form and no-form, that the most subtle of interventions within Chinese medicine take place.

The text continues with a description of the emergence of structure

---

3 Huainanzi chapter 7; Jing Shen, Monkey Press 2010, p. 3

from this primal chaos, which is full of potential:

> 'dark obscure
> formless soundless
> unfathomable profound
> Two spirits merge into life
> To regulate heaven and organize earth'

From this chaotic matrix two spirits or archetypal patterns emerge, and the elements of light and space begin to rise and disperse, those of darkness and heaviness to descend and coalesce. That which is light and dispersed is known as heaven, that which is heavy and solid is known as earth. These two spirits, often called Fuxi and Nugua, are in the realm of no-form, of patterning – and could be called the inherent laws of the universe which give rise to the expansion of heaven and the solid contraction that is the earth. In illustrations they are usually represented with compass and square to set the geometry and numerology on which the development of life is based.

Fig 1: Fuxi and Nugua holding compass and square

'…From this they divide into *yin yang*… and the ten thousand beings then take form.'

Yin and *yang* represent the powers of heaven and earth – the ability to sink and contract and to rise and expand – and the way in which these two forces intermingle to allow the formation of life according to each individual pattern. The ten thousand beings or things (a way to describe 'everything under the sun') arise from nothingness, organized and regulated according to their inherent laws and principles, and exist until those principles unravel and there is a return to nothingness, to no-form (*wu xing* 無 形). Life is an emergence from the one, death a re-absorption back into the one. The *dao* is the process or grace by which this all takes place.

YIN YANG

The two archetypal principles of Fuxi and Nugua manifest themselves in the real world – in the lives of the ten thousand beings and things – through the interaction of *yin* and *yang*. All life can be described as a dynamic interpenetration and mingling of *yin* and *yang*, as expressed in the Lüshi Chunqiu:

'The great unity (*tai yi* 太一) brings forth the two principles (*liang yi* 兩儀), the two principles bring forth *yin yang*. *Yin yang* change and transform, the one rising the other falling, joined together in a perfect pattern. Spinning and pulsing – if dispersed they rejoin, if joined they disperse again. This is called the invariable principle of nature (heaven, *tian* 天). …The ten thousand things emerge from the great unity and are transformed by *yin yang*.'[4]

Yin and *yang* are the great movements of life – opposite and yet as mutually inter-dependent as inhalation and exhalation. They operate from the most minute and personal to the cosmic or universal; their attraction and repulsion providing the rhythmic pulsation of life.

The oldest descriptions of the characters for *yin* and *yang* give their meaning as the sunny (*yang* 陽) and shady (*yin* 陰) side of a hill; one light and warm, the other shady and cold. This link with nature and the movement of the sun over the landscape suggests that the demarcation between what may be considered *yin* and what may be considered *yang* is constantly changing according to the time of day, the season of the year.

Etymologically, both characters share the same root, or radical, which is the part of the character which sets it into a context. The radical for both *yin* and *yang* (阝) has the meaning of the side of a hill. Each character has a different phonetic part, on the right, which gives the pronunciation and also sheds more light on the meaning. The phonetic of the *yin* character suggests an accumulation of mist and clouds (侌); the phonetic part of the *yang* character, the sun (日) rising above the horizon (一) and stimulating movement (勿).[5]

One of the earliest uses of these two characters was to describe and

---

4 Yin Yang in Classical Texts, Monkey Press 2006, p. 45

5 ibid. p 1

contrast the rising of the sun during the day bringing warmth and light, and its decline into darkness and cold. This also suggests an expansion and extension with the *yang*, and a contraction and consolidation with the *yin*. Within this was an understanding of their cyclical nature, of their alternation, one decreasing as the other comes into prominence. By the 4th century BCE they were commonly used to describe the rhythms of day and night and the changing of the seasons: *yin* becomes synonymous with cold and darkness, *yang* with light and warmth.

In many of the most ancient texts, an appropriate balance and communion of *yin yang* suggests good fortune, whereas an imbalance may result in all kinds of disasters. In the Guo Yu (Discourses of the Kingdoms), the State of Zhou has experienced a series of earthquakes. They are described in the text as an imbalance of the *yin* and *yang*, where the *yang* is trapped within rather than expanding and circulating in its natural way.[6]

The ability to determine the balance of *yin* and *yang* within the natural world – and by extension, within the human body – was considered vital for any kind of diagnosis and treatment:

'Nature (heaven, *tian* 天) produces *yin yang*, cold and heat, wet and dry, the transformations (*hua* 化) of the four seasons and the changes (*bian* 變) of the myriad things. Each of these can produce benefit (*li* 利) or harm (*hai* 害). The sage scrutinizes what is appropriate to the *yin* and *yang* and discriminates what is beneficial for the ten thousand things in order to enhance life (*bian sheng* 便 生).'[7]

---

6 Guo Yu, Discourses of the Kingdoms, in Yin Yang in Classical Texts, p 13

7 Lüshi Chunqiu Book 3, chapter 2, in Yin Yang in Classical Texts, p 49

Early descriptions of *yin yang* express the two great movements of life generated by the interaction and interpenetration of heaven and earth, as seen in the constant warming and cooling, ascending and descending of vapours as heat expands and cold contracts. These movements and changes within the atmosphere are often described as the 'eight winds' – which fill the 'eight extremities' or eight directions of the space between heaven and earth. Later these winds came to be known as *qi* (氣), and as the concept of *qi* evolved, descriptions of the interaction of *yin qi* and *yang qi* became central to the formation of an understanding of the movement and development of life.

The arts of both *feng shui* (風 水) and Chinese medicine are based on an ability to discern the patterns and movements of *yin* and *yang* both in nature and within the body. *Feng shui* (literally wind water) deals with mountains and rivers, and the way that wind and water both mould the landscape and show us its inner structure, whereas Chinese medicine addresses what is often referred to as the inner landscape, the mountains and rivers of the human body – the physical structure formed and maintained by the inner forces of wind and water, *qi* and blood.

Within the Yijing (易 經, I Ching, Book of Changes) – generally considered the most ancient of the great classic texts of China – the changes from *yin* to *yang*, *yang* to *yin* are symbolic of the way that life proceeds; *yang* is used to describe activity and *yin* passivity; *yang* to represent the action of heaven, which moves and stirs things into being, *yin* the action of earth, which consolidates and conserves. *Yang* is represented by a solid line (–) and *yin* by a broken line (--). In combination these broken and unbroken lines make the four images, eight trigrams and 64 hexagrams. Each hexagram is a different combination of six *yin* and *yang* lines. The succession and interaction of these *yin* and *yang* lines are considered to represent all possible human situations, and the movement and unfolding of the *yin yang* lines to give insight into the most appropriate action in a given situation.

In all these various examples of their use, *yin* and *yang* always maintain their relationship to the basic patterns and interactions of heaven and earth, and describe the way in which various beings and things take form. Each being and thing has its own pattern of *yin yang*, determined by its individual information patterning – which could be called its *qi* pattern.

Yin and yang qi

The character for *qi* (氣) – literally steam or vapours – is seen in early bronze inscriptions as synonymous with the wind. It was originally used to describe the exchanges and interchanges of influences that occur between heaven and earth – wind and rain, heat and cold, and various other types of weather. In early calendars, each season was described as having a specific type of *qi* – warm or cool, misty or clear, damp or dry.

What was referred to in the Huainanzi as *xiang* (象), a pattern or model of potential in the realm of no-form, is held and maintained by an intermingling of *yin qi* and *yang qi* in the realm of form. *Qi* acts as a kind of intermediary between form and formlessness.

The correct balance of *qi* is described in terms of *yin* and *yang* – each must be in their correct place, but free to move and circulate – the stagnation of *qi* being seen as the most dangerous situation, whether in nature, as we saw with the example of the earthquake, or when applied to the health of the body. Life is maintained by the harmonious blending of *yin yang qi,* as we see in the continuation of Laozi chapter 42:

'The ten thousand beings lean on the *yin* and embrace the *yang* and their powerful blending of *qi* makes harmony.'⁸

In popular language *qi* becomes synonymous with life-force – and in modern Japan the most common form of greeting is to ask about the state of one's *qi*.

The cycles and seasons of yin yang

From very early times *yin* and *yang* were used to describe the cycles of the day and of the year – the *yang* stirring into life at sunrise, and warming the earth towards midday, when there is a slow decline of light and heat as the day moves towards the *yin* times of sunset and midnight. In this text from the very first part of the Huangdi Neijing, the four seasons of the year are taken as a pattern for all natural cycles, and show that life is a process of cyclical change:

> 'The four seasons of *yin yang* are the end and the beginning of the ten thousand beings; the root of death and of life. Going against their succession destroys life. Going with their succession prevents illness. This is to obtain the way (*dao* 道).'⁹

Within the cycle of the four seasons, spring and summer are the *yang* months; the *qi* awakens and growth begins in spring and there is a flowering and fruition in the summer months. Autumn and winter are times of contraction and decline, as the *qi* moves within and the potential for life is buried within the ground. Dawn and spring are known as young

---

8 Laozi chapter 42 as quoted in Huainanzi chapter 7, Jing Shen, p. 7
9 Neijing Suwen chapter 2, The Way of Heaven, Monkey Press 1999, p. 137

yang (⚏), summer and midday as old *yang* (⚌), autumn and sunset as young *yin* (⚎), winter and midnight as old *yin* (⚏).

These four symbols are known as the four images (*si xiang* 四 象) and express the basic interaction and interpenetration of *yin* and *yang*. At the spring and autumn equinox, as well as at sunrise and sunset in the day, *yin* and *yang* are equal (as shown in the young *yin* and young *yang* symbols) but at sunrise *yang* is in ascendency, and full of power, while *yin* is in decline. At sunset and at the autumn equinox, *yin* is in ascendency and *yang* is in decline. (Fig. 2)

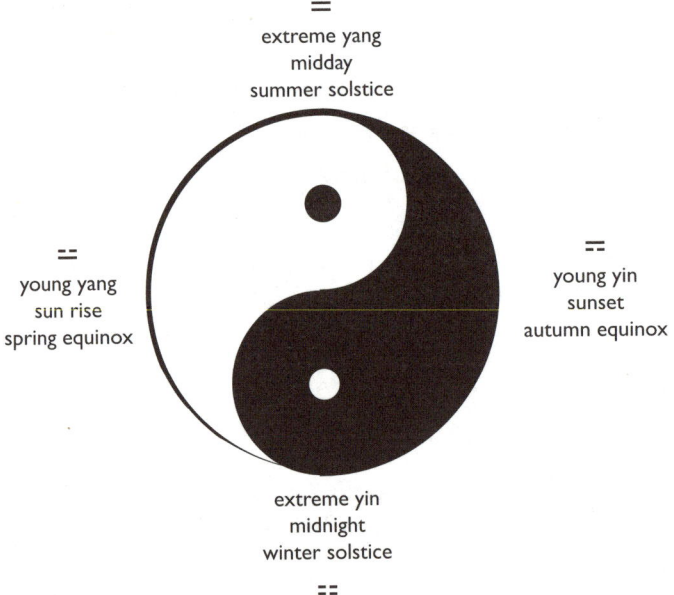

Fig 2: *The four seasons of yin yang*

Suwen chapter 2 describes how human beings can best preserve and maintain their *qi* by regulating their behaviour according to the *qi* of the four seasons. In the winter it is necessary to conserve, in the spring to move and stretch, in summer to relax – while being careful not to overheat, and in autumn to restrict and refine in preparation for the lean months of winter.

'In the seasons we can see the unfolding and progress of time, and time is nothing other than a succession and movement of different qualities of *qi*. The same succession and movement occurs within the human body in order to organize and maintain life.'[10]

WU XING

The definition of the movement of life in terms of *yin* and *yang* and the four seasons is further elaborated in the *wu xing* (五 行) – the five elements, phases or movements. *Wu xing* theory was very clearly defined by the time of the Early Han dynasty, but it is a concept which slowly evolved throughout the first millennium BCE. One of the earliest descriptions of five substances (at this time often called *wu cai* 五 材) is

---

10 Elisabeth Rochat de la Vallée, The Lung, Monkey Press, 2001, p. 5

found in a text of the 5th century BCE, the Spring and Autumn Annals (Chunqiu Zuozhuan):

> 'Heaven produces five basic raw materials (*wu cai* 五 材); their use is necessary for people to live. If one were lacking, people would be unable to survive.'[11]

An understanding of these five basic raw materials – water, fire, wood, metal and earth – was seen as vital for human life on earth. It was considered important to understand how each element behaved, and a knowledge of water, for example, would imply a knowledge of the maintenance of rivers and lakes, knowing how to fish without depleting stock; that of wood, the maintenance of forests and working and building with wood; the mining and forging of metals – earth, a knowledge of farming. So the early concept of *wu xing* provided an ecological understanding of the world – supplying the knowledge to live sustainably and in accordance with nature.

A description of the nature of these five substances appears in the Hongfan, or Great Plan, which is a part of the Book of Documents. It seems simple enough – but a great importance is attached to these attributes and we will see that they have a far-reaching influence on medical theory.

> 'Water soaks and descends, fire burns and ascends, wood bends and straightens, metal yields and changes, earth receives seeds and gives crops.'[12]

---

[11] Wu Xing: The Five Elements in Classical Chinese Texts, Monkey Press 2009, p. 5

[12] ibid. p. 27

Within the Hongfan it is explained that the nature of the five substances must be studied in depth in order to manage them well. This is often illustrated by the story of an official named Gun. Gun was put in charge of the management of waterways and grew in favour in the courts as his plans to build a series of dykes to accommodate the annual flooding of the Yellow River came to fruition. For some nine years his plan seemed to work, but then there was a great flood which destroyed the dykes and caused devastation on a scale that had never been seen before. His son, Yu (who came to be known as Yu the Great), explained that the damming of the water goes against its innate nature – which is to soak and descend. He therefore built a series of drainage ditches, which allowed the water to flow away – a system which has been successfully replicated until recent times.[13]

The story of Gun – who was exiled and possibly executed – is used to stress the importance of following the natural movement of things, and not to go against their intrinsic nature. Water behaves in a particular way, and to go against that is to go against the natural order of life – against the *dao*, and will eventually cause calamities. According to this understanding, the damming of great rivers could certainly produce an imbalance within the earth's equilibrium possibly causing land shift and earthquakes – as was illustrated in the Guo Yu.

By the time of the Huangdi Neijing, the theory of the five elements had expanded to provide an archetypal representation of the natural ordering of things – and while remaining based in the qualities of these five basic elements, the theory of *wu xing* became central to a cosmology which explained the world in terms of qualities and movements of *qi*. The school of Yinyang Wuxing was firmly established in the 2nd century

---

13 ibid. p. 21

BCE and formed the basis for the theoretical infrastructure of classical Chinese medicine.

Both in the medical texts and in other literature of the time, the energetic qualities of the five elements are illustrated by the movement of *qi* throughout the four seasons. The *yang* qualities of light and heat are attributed to the element fire, the *yin* qualities of cold and darkness to water. Being warm and light, fire has a rising movement, it is related to the quality of *qi* in the summer; water is cold and dark and has a descending movement, and is related to the *qi* of winter.

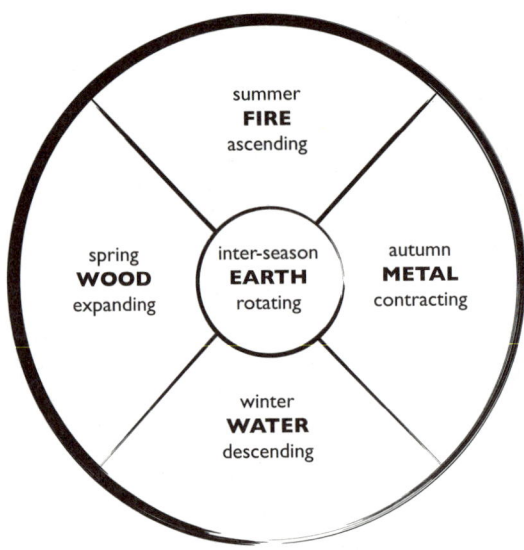

Fig 3: the five elements/phases, asociated seasons and movement of qi

Fire and water are the primal elements, as they most clearly illustrate the qualities of *yin* and *yang* within the phenomenological world. Wood and metal include both *yin* and *yang* qualities; according to the Hongfan, wood is able both to bend and be straight – it has the yielding quality of bamboo, which bends with the wind, but also the strength and hardness to make gates and doors; the endurance to make a boat which will last for years – but which also has the ability to float. Metal is the hardest substance, and is used to forge weapons, but it can also change shape – it can be melted down again and again and reformed.

Within the year, wood and metal are related to the spring and autumn. In spring the *yang* is rising, there is a movement from the dark depths of winter which expands outwards – seeds sprout, plants begin to grow. This is the time of wood energy which can be violent but always dynamic. It is fast, changeable, and is often expressed by the movement of the wind. Metal is related to autumn, when the *yang* is withdrawing, there is a concentration and condensation into the depths of the earth; a weighing up and a letting go in preparation for the harshness of the winter months.

The fifth element is earth, and in the Chinese calendar it is given the position of the centre, the activity of rotation. It is the earth which provides the basis for the other elements, but also allows their movement and change. The cycle of the year moves around the element earth, and at each inter-seasonal point, there are 16 days which are governed by the *qi* of the earth. The *qi* of the earth allows the correct intermingling and exchange of *qi* between spring and summer, summer and autumn, autumn and winter, winter and spring. These passages of time are called the gates of the year – and have a correspondence with the cross-quarter days of the Celtic calendar.

The four gates of the year have a particular quality of *qi*, and in the calendar they are marked by festivals, the exact timing of which traditionally depends on the phase of the moon. Chinese new year is celebrated at the gate between winter and spring and is called heaven's gate; it is a celebration of the return of light and life after the winter months. The time between spring and summer is called the people's gate

– and, as in the Celtic May Day, is a celebration of fertility and the entwining of the energies of heaven and earth, male and female, which is expressed in the traditional maypole dances in Europe. In Japan it is children's day. The movement between summer and autumn is the gate of earth, celebrated in both Eastern and Western cultures by the first harvest. At the end of autumn is the gate of ghosts – the time when the *qi* of the earth is contracting and descending, and the veil between the worlds of the living and the dead is especially thin.

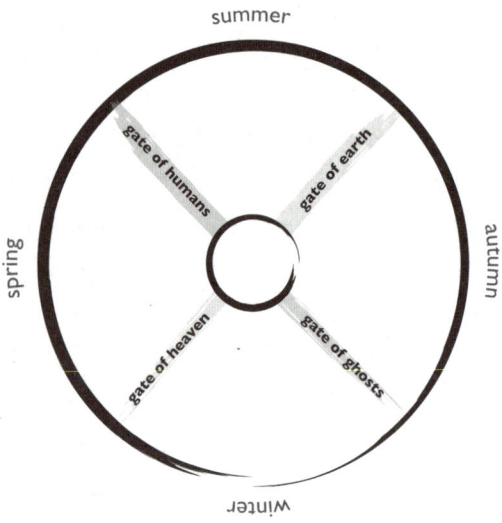

Fig 4: the gates of the year

Wu xing theory, whether translated as the five elements, five phases or five movements, essentially describes the five different ways in which *qi* moves and behaves, and this traditional understanding of the five elements based on the cycles of the year is a practical and useful way of understanding what can sometimes seem rather obscure and counterintuitve information. Within medical theory, these five movements of *qi* are reflected in the actions and functions of the five internal organs. Descriptions of their energetic patterns are based on this understanding of the seasonal *qi*, in much the same way that classical Greek medicine of the same time used the patterns of the seasons as a basis for its own system of elements and humours, which was then elaborated into distinctions between types of people and appropriate treatments.

This system of correspondence also relates the elements to climates and to the four directions (fig 5): water is related to the cold climate and by extension to the north, which is cold and dark. The fire element is related to heat and to the south – which is associated with light and heat. The wood element is associated with the wind, and the rising of the sun, and therefore it is linked to the east. Metal is related to dryness, to the lessening of the light, and therefore to the setting sun and the west. In the same way that the earth element does not have a specific season (though in some texts it is related to the late summer, and the time of harvest) – it also has no specific direction, but is related to the centre. It is central both in position and function, and its climate is dampness, reflecting the fertility of the earth and a productive balance of fire and water.

As *yin* and *yang* describe the fundamental pulsation and rhythm of the *qi* inwards and outwards – the in-breath and the out-breath, contraction and expansion, materialization and dissolution – the movements of the five elements or phases qualify this further with the vital outward movement of the wood element, the gentle upward movement of fire, the turning within and condensing of the metal and the descending of water – all harmonized by the rotation of the earth. These five basic movements of the *qi* are seen in action within the five *zang* (the internal organs and their dependent functions), their smooth functioning and interaction ensuring health, their lack of harmony the basis of pathology.

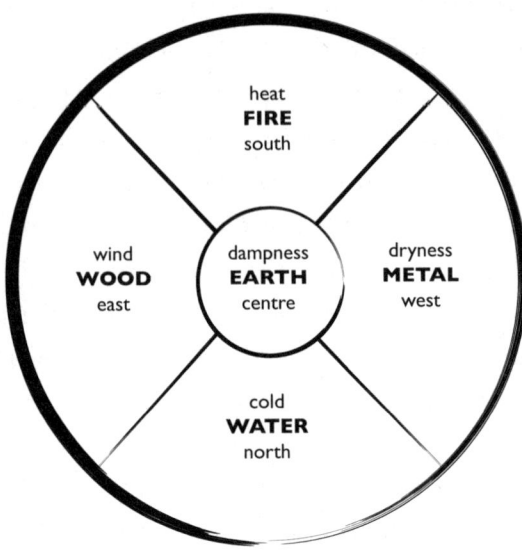

Fig 5: The five elements; associated climates and directions

So the concept of the five elements (*wu xing* 五 行) further elaborates the way in which beings and things come into form – *yin yang* provides the basic patterning for material manifestation, the five elements further describe the five (*wu* 五) elemental ways in which *qi* moves and acts (*xing* 行). These movements or actions of *qi* have a specific resonance or vibration which sets up a particular kind of *qi* patterning. Each element, for example, has a musical note and a colour – which vibrate at a certain frequency. As sand on a tray forms patterns in response to a musical note, so the *qi* pattern responds to the different resonances of the five elements – and the *qi* can be tuned by employing the vibration of sound, colour, the intrinsic qualities of food, specific ritual dance or movements – and of course by the use of the acupuncture needle. The systematic correspondences or resonances of the five elements, found in modern text books as well as the classical literature, refer to this idea of mutual resonance – and it is vital when looking at these lists and tables to remember that they refer to a quality and movement of *qi*.

THE THREE TREASURES *jing qi shen*

We came across the notion of *qi* in the context of *yin yang*, but in order to understand its function within human beings, it is important to consider its place within what are often called the three treasures (*san bao* 三 寶) – so-called because they are the most precious attributes of life and must be protected with care.

Jing (精) *qi* (氣) and *shen* (神) reflect the most essential nature of a human being – living, as we have seen, between the influences of heaven and earth, endowed with a true nature (*xing* 性) and an inherited fate or destiny (*ming* 命). The true nature manifests itself through the *shen*, spirit; inherited tendencies manifest themselves through the *jing*, essence. These two are mediated by the *qi*.

SHEN

The character *shen* (神) dates back to the Shang dynasty, where it has been discovered on ancient bronzes related to shamanic practices of divination and ancestor worship. It is a character made of two parts – that on the left (示) signifies a manifestation of power from above, and was used in early times with the meaning of an altar. The right part conveys the idea of extension (申), and more specifically the extension and bestowal of beneficial influence. In early societies, this character was used to mean 'beneficial influences coming from heaven'. Within a shamanic view of the world, it suggests a kind of supplication to heavenly or ancestral powers to intervene in earthly affairs.

In the early texts, *shen* may be found paired with *gui* (鬼) – where the *shen* are spirits of heaven, *gui* the spirits of earth; in certain contexts, the *shen* bring good fortune, *gui* bad fortune. *Gui* are sometimes portrayed as hungry ghosts which feed on human desires, whereas the *shen* are attracted by the purity and stillness of the human heart and mind. The daoist sages suggest 'sitting quietly doing nothing' to calm the heart/mind and attract the *shen*, in order to cultivate the true nature.

During the 5th and 4th centuries BCE, Daoist and Confucian philosophers began to understand the *shen* as the enlightened human consciousness – that aspect of the human being able to seek something other, something greater – to aspire towards the unknown. The *shen* always remain part of the unchanging unity – before the division into *yin* and *yang* – and as such have a natural tendency to return. As we find in the commentary on the Yijing, the Xici:

'That which is beyond the *yin yang* is called *shen*.'[14]

The *shen* are a bit of heavenly unity within us. Their main quality is to illuminate (*shen ming* 神 明) – they bring clarity and illumination to the perception, enlighten consciousness, make seeing, hearing, and all awareness, acute.

'The way to purity is to guard the spirit (*shen* 神), this alone; guard it, and never lose it, and you will become one with spirit, one with its pure essence (*jing* 精).'[15]

JING

Jing and *shen* make up an interdependent, interpenetrating couple. The left part (米), the radical of the character *jing* (精) is shared with *qi* (氣) – and has the meaning of ripe grain bursting with vitality. The right part (青) is the colour of growing vegetation, a kind of green blue, which is not so much a colour but a sign of life. It can be used to describe

---

14 Yin Yang in Classical Texts, p. 67

15 Zhuangzi chapter 15

the complexion, the shine of the hair, a sparkle in the eyes – anything that conveys life and vitality. *Jing* (精) has the meaning of both vitality and essence – because when related to substance it is the most refined and subtle – it is the essential nature of things. Its original meaning was that of the finest ground grains, which provide the best nourishment and are the most easily assimilated.

Within the human body, *jing* is the most refined, the most subtle of material substances. It may also refer to sexual essence, sperm and ova. It relates to inherited tendencies and the informational patterning received through ancestry. *Jing* is received at conception, directs development and growth, both in the embryo, and in adult life in order that we may fulfil our allotted life-span – if we inherit a good quality of *jing*, and we do not abuse it, we may enjoy good health and longevity.

Jing (精) and *shen* (神) interpenetrate to provide the basis for human life. *Jing* provides the original patterning – through the *ming* (命 – our allotted life energy received from our parents) – and *shen* gives the aspiration to each individual human life, through the *xing* (性) – our true nature. The term *jing shen* is used to refer to the life force, the vital spirit – and is found in the early philosophical literature to define the most inner and most precious aspects of a human being. We will return to these terms again and again in the elaboration of medical theory, where *jing shen* remains the basis of all human life – mediated and animated by the *qi*.

> '*Jing* is the living fabric of the universe, the element of life which is transformed and put in motion by the *qi*.' [16]

---

16 Essence Spirit Blood and Qi, Monkey Press 1999, p. 31

QI

Qi moves and transforms. Like the wind, it could be said to have no innate qualities of its own, it merely responds to external circumstances. In nature, high and low pressure systems stimulate the movement of air, which takes on the quality of the land over which it travels, becoming heavy and damp, or light and dry. Warm air will rise, cold air will sink – and it is much the same with *qi* within the body. *Qi* is given different names and different functions, one changing to another, according to circumstance and location. What is most important is that it can move freely, without blockage or stagnation, enabling the many changes and transformations which occur constantly within the human body.

Qi follows certain pathways – it flows with the blood, it flows in the interstitial tissues, it resides in each of the organs and regulates the movement along the digestive tract. All of these particular locations and functions of the *qi* are given specific names – though it is always important to remember that *qi* is also simply *qi*.

Yuan Qi

Yuan qi (原 氣) is the original *qi*, the *qi* which is closest to the origins of life. The character *yuan* (原) depicts a water source, or spring, and *yuan qi* retains the connection to the source throughout all the changes and interchanges of *qi* within the body, which are often described with images of water, as springs, marshes, pools, rivers and seas. It is closely related to the *jing*, essence, and both *yuan qi* and *jing* carry our original imprint and patterning – *yuan qi* ensuring that throughout the many changes and re-formations that take place within the body, we remain essentially the same. It acts as a kind of catalyst, maintaining the continuity with our original inheritance in all exchanges and transformations. In comparing *jing* and *yuan qi*, *jing* has the *yin* quality of preservation, while *yuan qi* has the *yang* quality of transformation.

Zong Qi

Zong qi (宗氣), generally translated as either gathering or ancestral *qi*, is the combination of original *qi* with the *qi* acquired from food and breath. According to Western science, our bodies break down food into the most subtle substance, which when combined with oxygen is metabolized into usable energy. This is much the same as the Chinese view. The most subtle essences of food (*jing wei* 精味) combine with the *qi* of the lungs (the breath) and with the catalytic action of the *yuan qi* become usable energy (*zong qi* 宗氣). The *zong qi* is said to gather in the centre of the chest at the 'sea of *qi*', where its regular pulsation provides rhythm to the beating of the heart.

The classical meaning of *zong* (宗) is a kind of clan gathering of ancestors, and the gathering of the *qi* in the chest has this idea of bringing together what is naturally part of our original pattern and rejecting that which is not. It may be a primitive attempt to describe immunity, and the ability to discriminate between what belongs to the body and what needs to be expelled. That information is based in the original *qi*

Qi is distributed around the body from the 'sea of *qi*' in the chest through a network of connections and circulations; it is found in the blood vessels where it moves and invigorates the circulation of blood; in the interstitial tissues where it follows specific pathways, or ways of least resistance, called channels and meridians. It acts at the surface of the skin where it is called defensive *qi* (*wei qi* 衛 氣) and supplies nutrients to the cells as nutritional or reconstructive *qi* (*ying qi* 營 氣).[17]

Blood and Qi

> 'The ebb and flow of the *qi* corresponds with heaven and earth, with its four seasons and five elements. The increase and decline in the power of the *mai* (脈 pulse) are the observation of emptiness and fullness, excess and deficiency of the blood and *qi*.[18]

We saw that *jing shen* come together to form the most essential aspects of human life – they are described as a precious gift, which can be received and treasured, but not altered or replenished. Blood and *qi* (*xue qi* 血 氣) form a *yin yang* couple within the physical body and are the basis for all diagnosis and treatment within Chinese medicine. As practitioners it is the blood and *qi* that we work with, and it is by enhancing the blood and *qi* that it is possible to create an environment within which the *jing shen* thrive. Within this couple, *qi* is *yang*, it has no form and provides movement, warmth and stimulation; blood is *yin*, it has substance and provides nutrients and moisture. *Qi* is said to move, hold and guide the blood within the vessels.

---

17 cf. Essence Spirit Blood and Qi; A Study of Qi, Monkey Press 2008
18 Lingshu chapter 55, in Essence Spirit Blood and Qi, p. 83

Yin and yang qi in medicine

Qi may also be described simply as *yin* and *yang qi*, following the archetypal *yin yang* relationship within the body. *Yang qi* moves and warms. It has an outward centrifugal action, dispersing towards the exterior. *Yin qi* seeks coalition, it moves inwards, binding, creating shape and form. These two intertwine, hold on to each other, keep each other stable. *Yin* stops *yang* floating away, *yang* stops *yin* becoming inert.

Within the human body, *yin* represents the building and maintenance of structures, the ability to nourish, to conserve, to be still and keep precious substances within. *Yin* is all that is hidden and deep, *yang* that which moves outwards and protects; each one dependent on the other. As we see in Suwen chapter 3:

> 'From ancient times, the communication with heaven, the foundation of life, has been rooted in *yin yang*... Thus the *yang* soars upwards and ensures defence at the exterior...
> That which gives life to the *yin* is rooted in the five tastes (*wu wei* 五味); *yin* is that which treasures (*cang* 藏) the essences, then there can be springing up and development [of life] (*qi ji* 起 亟).
> *Yang* is that which defends on the exterior (*wei wai* 衛 外) and then solidity is the result...
> *Yin* is inside (*nei* 內) but *yang* guards it (*shou* 守). *Yang* is outside (*wai* 外) but *yin* sends it (*shi* 使).'[19]

This passage illustrates the constant movement and interaction of *yin* and *yang*. While guarding the exterior, *yang* also ensures containment, nothing is lost; *qi* and fluids are retained and returned to the *yin*. *Yang* is able to

---

19 Yin Yang in Classical Texts, p. 83

reach and protect the exterior because of its rooting within the *yin*.

The functions of *yin* and *yang qi* are stated very simply in Suwen chapter 5:

'*Yang* transforms the *qi*; *yin* completes the form.'[20]

Yin and *yang* may be used to describe all possible expressions within the body. At every level, *yin yang* gives the basic understanding and differentiation. In Chinese medicine, all pathology is an imbalance of *yin yang*, all diagnosis a measurement of this imbalance, all treatment a rectification.

20 ibid. p. 112

THE INTERNAL ORGANS: THE FIVE ZANG

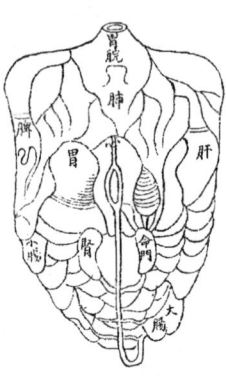

Ming dynasty illustration of the internal organs showing the lung 肺, *heart* 心, *liver* 肝, *stomach* 胃, *spleen* 脾, *kidneys* 腎, *ming men* 命 門, *small* 小 *and large intestines* 大 腸.

Within Chinese medicine, the internal organs are separated into two groups, the organs which have a *yin* function of storage (*cang* 藏) and the organs which have a *yang* function of transportation (*chuan* 傳) and transformation (*hua* 化) of food. The *yin* organs are the kidneys, the liver, the heart, the spleen and the lung; the *yang* organs the stomach, small and large intestines, the gallbladder, the bladder and a function known as the triple heater, or the three warming spaces.

The five *yin* organs, the *zang* (臟) – which means to store and to treasure (藏) within the body (肉/月) – are closely related to the five elements, and the early chapters of the Neijing Suwen define the basis of their functions and relationships. Chapter 2 ('Adjusting the *qi* in accordance with the *qi* of the four seasons') provides a link between the internal organs and the *qi* of a season, suggesting, for example, that failing to adjust and act according to the *qi* of winter will cause damage to the kidneys.

In Suwen chapters 4 and 5, this is further elaborated, and the *qi* of the season, and of each element, is described as resonating with a particular organ and its related functions. We will begin by looking closely at each of the five *zang*, drawing where appropriate on these four season/five element relationships, which are always based on an understanding of *yin yang* and the natural movement of *qi*.

In discussing the five *zang*, it is important to remember that although we use the translation of kidneys for the character *shen* (腎), for example, its meaning within Chinese medicine is much broader and includes a wide range of functions beyond the scope of the genito-urinary system within Western medicine. The sphere of influence of each *zang* includes its associated meridian pathways, and various physical, emotional and mental tendencies which may be governed by its particular movement of *qi*. As we look in turn at each of the five *zang*, we will use the early chapters of the Suwen to illustrate their physiology.

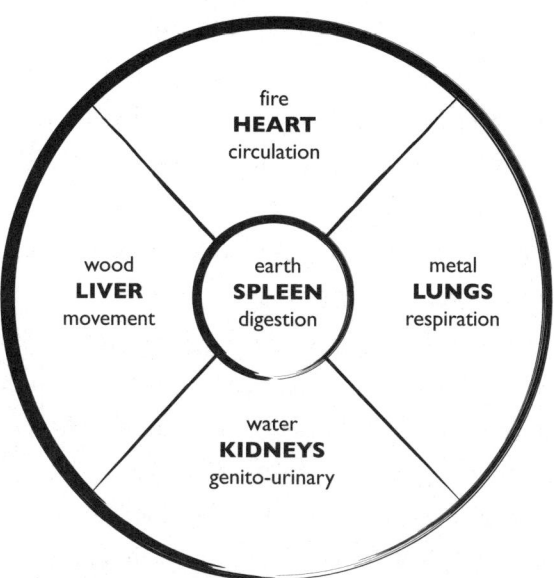

Fig 6: Elements and related organ systems; wu xing and wu zang

WATER AND THE KIDNEYS

The water element is related to winter. In winter *qi* moves downwards and inwards; its climate is cold. Suwen chapter 2 describes this activity of the *qi* in winter as the 'maintenance and preservation of life'. It is in the depths of the winter that life is stored deep within – there is a retraction, a drawing in, a conservation. This movement also describes the action of the kidney *qi* within the body: it is located in the lower abdomen, within the belly, it draws downwards and concentrates. And as seeds of new life are stored deep within the earth throughout the winter months, so the kidneys, within the Chinese medical model, include in their sphere of influence the seeds of fertility. The kidneys (*shen* 腎) are said to 'store the essence, (*jing* 精)', which refers to the subtle essences coming from the origin, but also to sperm and ovum.

We saw in the Hongfan that water 'soaks and descends'. Within this text, water is the primary element, and the kidneys are the *zang* most closely connected to the origin, to the original *qi* and the beginnings of life. They are responsible for maintaining the patterning, through the *jing* and the *yuan qi*, both for the life of an individual and for passing on the information patterning through sperm and ovum.

The first chapter of the Suwen describes the life-cycles of men and women in terms of their fertility. For both men and women, the first stage of the cycle describes the 'rising power of the *qi* of the kidneys'. At each stage of the seven year (for women) and eight year (for men) cycles, the kidney *qi* rises in power, at each stage both vitality and fertility increase, until the cycles reverse and as vitality declines, fertility decreases. For example:

'At seven years, the kidney *qi* of a woman rises in power...

'At eight times eight years, the fertility of a man declines; sperm (*jing* 精) is less, the kidneys decline in power...'[21]

The quality of the essences and the power of the kidneys to store thus define both fertility and the ageing process – the maintenance and preservation of life.

'...This is the way that is natural to the *qi* of winter, which corresponds to the maintenance and preservation of life. To go against this would injure the kidneys, causing weakening in spring, through an insufficient contribution to the generation of life.'[22]

The kidneys, and hence the fertility, are damaged by cold, so care is taken to ensure that the lower abdomen is kept warm, especially in the case of women. Within Chinese medicine, many cases of miscarriage or inability to conceive may be diagnosed as due to 'cold uterus'. Suwen chapter 2 describes the behaviour appropriate to the winter months as conserving energy, keeping warm, going to bed early, getting up late – acting in accordance with the available daylight hours. Depletion of the kidneys requires rest and restoration because they are the basis of physical

---

21 Suwen chapter 1, in The Way of Heaven, p. 67, 85
22 Suwen chapter 2 as quoted in The Kidneys, Monkey Press 2001, p. 49. See The Way of Heaven for the complete text of Neijing Suwen chapters 1 and 2.

life and strength. In order for the kidney *qi* to be strong and powerful, it is necessary to act in accordance with the *qi* of the winter – to conserve, to maintain, to be rooted in the depths of the being.

The kidneys govern the li (裡)

In Suwen chapter 52, the kidneys are said to 'govern the *li*'.[23] The *li* (裡) here refers both to the innermost structures and the movement of the *qi* towards the depths of the body. It is the responsibility of the kidneys to draw down and conserve. They govern the deep structuration and provide a foundation and grounding for life. The firm basis provided by the kidney *qi* manifests itself both physically and psychologically. The grounding and rooting of the kidney *qi* is also seen in the mind and emotions, and the emotions are often described as the first expression of the movement of *qi* within a human being.

On the physical level, the ability of the kidneys to provide inner stability is reflected in their association with both bones and marrow in Suwen chapter 5. This important text describes the five phase resonances of each of the *zang* with its associated direction, climate, main sphere of influence within the body, its associated emotions and so on. The section relating to water and the kidneys begins:

> 'The northern quadrant produces cold
> cold produces water
> water produces the salty taste
> the salty taste produces the kidneys

---

23 The Kidneys, p. 4

the kidneys produce bones and marrow.'[24]

We have already seen the connection between water, the north and the cold, and here in Suwen chapter 5 water is said to produce the salty taste. Each of the elements has an associated taste, an idea which dates back to the earliest texts. Each taste stimulates a reaction and movement in the *qi*, and each taste – or the chemical constituents of a particular food – resonates with specific systems of the body. The text of the Hongfan says that water 'moistens and descends', and the next sentence brings the association with the salty taste – simply 'that which moistens and descends produces saltiness'.[25] Salt is produced by the evaporation of water, which leaves mineral deposits. It is heavy in nature. The salty taste has the action of descending and coalescing within the body. In Chinese herbal medicine, the salty taste is often related to the minerals found in seaweeds and the shells of shellfish. We can imagine quite easily the relationship between minerals, a movement of concentration, and the structure of the bones, but within Chinese herbal medicine, minerals may also be used to ground the psyche, to give more substance and weight where that is seen to be lacking.

The bones give the body its ability to be upright and stable, and provide the firm basis that is vital to the functioning of the kidneys. The bones are hard and give structure, the marrow soft, moistening and nourishing. Bone and marrow therefore form a kind of *yin yang* couple, a pattern which is often seen within the sphere of the kidneys. The brain is called 'the sea of marrow', and both the spine and brain are closely associated with kidney function. This again reflects the idea of the 'innermost' both

---

24 The Kidneys, p. 54. See The Rhythm at the Heart of the World, Monkey Press 2011, for a complete translation of Suwen chapter 5.

25 Wu Xing: The Five Elements in Classical Chinese Texts, p. 32

structurally, and as being close to the centre of life.

Suwen chapter 9 reflects the same ideas:

'The kidneys control hibernation and protect storage.
They are the residence of the essences.
Their flourishing aspect is the hair,
the power of their fullness is in the bones.'[26]

Teeth and hair

The text of Suwen 9 suggests that the hair is also associated with the kidneys, and in Chinese society, thick lustrous hair is a sign of a strong inherited vitality. The seven and eight year cycles of fertility in Suwen chapter 1 describe the rise and fall of the power of the kidney *qi* and this is often illustrated by the growth of the hair and the strength of the teeth, which are the visible aspect of the bones:

'A woman of seven years, the kidney *qi* rise in power, teeth are renewed and the hair grows…'

'A man of eight times eight years, fertility is exhausted, sperm (*jing* 精) are depleted, the kidneys decline, the hair and teeth begin to fall out.'[27]

The condition of the teeth and the hair is used here as an indication

---

26 The Kidneys, p. 51

27 ibid. p. 38-39

of the strength of the kidney *qi*. They are another example of a *yin yang* couple associated with the kidneys; the hair is soft and supple, the teeth hard and strong.

Colours, sounds, emotions

> '…of colours it is black
> of notes it is the note *yu*
> of sounds it is to sigh
> of reactive movements it is to shiver
> …of expressions of emotion it is fear.'

Returning to this section of Suwen chapter 5, black is the colour of darkness, of night and also of deep water. In medical diagnosis it may appear on the skin, especially under the eyes, as a sign of depletion of the kidney *qi*. Each note of the Chinese pentatonic scale resonates with one of the five elements, here it is the fifth note which has a deep bass tone. In music therapy, the tones are used to balance the specific *qi*, and music may be composed with this particular aim in mind.

A sigh is a sound which comes from deep within the body. It is a deep exhalation, the opposite of the yawn, which is an inhalation, and which relates more to the *qi* of the lungs. An exhalation gets rid of the stale *qi* and stirs a movement of *qi* deep within the body. In this way it is similar to the shiver – which is the natural reaction to cold and is the body's attempt to stimulate circulation.

We will discuss the emotions in more depth in a later chapter, but here it is important to mention that the emotion fear is associated with the kidneys because it is seen to have a downward action on the *qi*:

'When there is fear the *qi* descends.'[28]

And whether this manifests itself physically in, for example, a movement of the bowels – a common reaction to extreme and acute physical fear – or in a general tendency to retreat within and not engage with life, it is the movement of *qi* and its effects on the physiology that is important.

These various external signs may be used in diagnosis to ascertain a particular pathology. If a patient constantly sighs, is sensitive to cold and shivers a lot – possibly appearing to be withdrawn, we need to consider the state of the kidney *qi*.

The ears

The following line of the text says that, 'of orifices, it is the ears'. Each organ of storage has a related orifice, and the relationship between the kidneys and the ears is generally said to be one of morphology: there are two of them and they have a similar shape. This could be seen as fanciful, and certainly some of the five element resonances are more easily understood than others, but shape, especially when related to growth and development, is significant. What determines shape? To the Chinese, a similarity in shape suggests a similarity in the quality of *qi*, and within the information patterning controlling their development. It is interesting that some of the strange connections and relationships made within Chinese medicine can be traced back to embryological development, where tissues of the same type and origin migrate through the body with foetal development.

In Suwen chapter 4, which also lists five element resonances, the

---

28 Suwen chapter 39 in The Seven Emotions, Monkey Press 1996, 2014, p. 81

kidneys are related to the lower orifices:

> 'The black aspect (*hei se* 黑 色) of the northern quarter penetrates to communicate with the kidneys; it opens its orifice at the two *yin* (lower orifices); it stores its essences in the kidneys.'[29]

The double organ

The text of Suwen 5 represents the kidneys in resonance with the water element, but they also have a relationship with fire, which is defined in the Nanjing, the Classic of Difficulties. In both difficulties 36 and 39 the kidneys are described as a 'double organ' with a double storage (*cang* 臟). Nanjing difficulty 36 defines this double function:

> 'On the right is *ming men*, on the left is the kidney. *Ming men* is the residence of *shen jing* the source of the *yuan qi*.'[30]

We have seen that *ming* (命) is the inherited life energy, sometimes described as an 'allotted span of years' or a 'natural endowment'. *Men* (門) is a gate, and *ming men* is the gate through which inherited life enters and through which it is passed on. It is the source of *yuan qi*, the original *qi* which ensures our ability to remain true to our original information patterning. It stores *shen jing* (神 精), the vital spirits.

Nanjing difficulty 36 describes the right kidney as *ming men*, the left as the kidney. Left and right are generally seen here to be a symbolic reference to the *yin* and *yang* attributes of the kidney *qi*. In the early

---

29 Seminar notes

30 The Kidneys, p 9

classical texts the terms kidney *yin* and kidney *yang* are not mentioned, but this division between the fire and water aspects of the kidneys, between the water of the kidneys and the fire of *ming men,* are the forerunner of this later simplification.

Within the trigrams of the Yijing the water trigram, (*kan*) has two *yin* lines but in the centre is a *yang* line (☵) and this image is often used to illustrate the activity of kidney *qi* within the body, the central *yang* line representing the fire within the water. The trigram for fire (*li*) has two *yang* lines and a *yin* line at the centre (☲), suggesting that each is an intermingling of *yin* and *yang*. *Ming men* is the name of the acupuncture point on the primary *yang* channel (*du mai*) directly between the back *shu* points of the kidneys. This point on the spine at the level of the waist is the source of the fire in the lower abdomen, the spark of life within an area that is essentially *yin* in nature. *Ming men huo* (命 門 火), the fire of *ming men*, is a name often used for the fire in the lower abdomen which facilitates the transformation of *qi*.

The connection between the kidneys and reproduction is made clear as the text of Nanjing difficulty 36 continues:

'In men essences are stored; in women the uterus is attached.' (Fig 7)

The image of the *yang* within the *yin* is described again in Nanjing 66:

'The *qi* that moves between the kidneys, below the navel, is the life and destiny of a human being (*ren zhi sheng ming* 人 之 生 命). It is the root and foundation of the twelve meridians. Hence it is called the source (*yuan* 原).'[31]

---

31 Heart Master Triple Heater, Monkey Press 1998, p. 113

Fig. 7: Ming dynasty illustration to Nanjing difficulty 36, showing the hexagrams 63 and 64, After Completion and Before Completion. Both are made with the trigrams li and kan – fire and water. In hexagram 63 (below), fire is below, water above; in hexagram 64, water below, fire above. In the centre it says 'Fire and water become distinct.' Beneath the right kidney is the ideogram for fire, beneath the left, the ideogram for water. Beneath the right kidney, the text reads 'Man stores essences, jing (精)'; beneath the left kidney the text reads 'In women, the uterus (bao 胞) is attached.'

This pooling and vibration of original *qi* is the very source of life, and has an important part to play in fertility. It is the origin of each individual life, but also of the ability to create a new life. The balance of the fire and water of the kidneys create the right environment for both the conception and the growth and development of the child within the body of the mother – the *yin* aspect of the kidneys bringing nourishment and moistening which must be balanced by the appropriate warmth and movement of the *yang*. The quality of the sperm may be seen as an aspect of kidney *yin*, or the watery nature of the kidneys; the motility of the sperm more the *yang* or fire aspect of the kidneys.

These Nanjing texts bring us back to that basic attribute of the kidneys and the kidney *qi* – that they are close to the origins of life. The kidneys are responsible for fertility, for inherited tendencies, for early childhood and developmental diseases. They have a close relationship with sperm and to the uterus. They carry our patterning within the *jing* (精 essence).

Through their connection with the gate of life (命門 *ming men*) they are close to the original *qi* and to the root of the meridian system.

Controling the innermost aspects of the body, they ensure both the rooting of *qi* and the stability of the body form. The natural movement of water drawing inwards and downwards requires the constant balance of the fire for its movement and transformation. The kidneys control fluid balance, but it is the combination of water and fire in the lower abdomen which allows the proper dispersion of fluids around the body. The correct balance of fire and water, *yin* and *yang*, within the kidneys provides the correct degree of moistening with the ability to warm, diffuse and transform fluids, which might otherwise be retained, or unnecessarily expelled.

Fluid balance is controlled by the kidneys and their associated *fu* organ the bladder – but it is also assisted by the triple heater:

'The kidneys are connected to the bladder and the triple heater.'[32]

Each one of the five *zang* has a related *fu* organ, and once again the kidneys have a double association; whereas they are associated to the bladder as the *zang* and *fu* of the water element, they are also connected with the triple heater. This association may be said to be with *ming men* or kidney fire.

---

32 Lingshu chapter 47 in The Kidneys, p. 19

WOOD AND THE LIVER

According to the Hongfan, 'wood can both bend and be straight'. It can be supple and bend with the wind, but also strong and upright. Bamboo is often used to illustrate the wood *qi* – and in China it is highly regarded for its pliability and strength. It is strong enough to be used as a supporting scaffolding pole, but supple enough to bend and straighten again without snapping. And it is also hollow, so the wind can move through it. It is commonly used for flutes and pipes. The way that the air moves through a flute, making different notes according to the patterning of the fingers over the openings, is often compared to the emotions as they flow through the human being – they can be adjusted to make a pleasant tune in harmony with others, or create discord.

The wood element is related to the spring and the rising *yang*. Spring is the time of young *yang* energy – and the wood element is associated with the proliferation and growth of vegetation at this time of the year. After the inner containment of the water element during the winter months, the movement of the wood element in the spring is to expand and spread out; to move upwards and outwards. The young *yang* stirs things into life, both at dawn after sleep and in the spring, after the hibernation and withdrawal of winter. It is related to the east, where the sun rises, and to the wind, which agitates and stirs things into motion. Suwen chapter 2 describes this activity of the spring:

'The three months of spring are called springing up (*fa* 發) and unfolding; heaven and earth together produce life, and the ten thousand beings are invigorated.'[33]

After their separation during the winter months, a time of hibernation and withdrawal, the *qi* of heaven and earth come together to reproduce and reinvigorate life. The character *fa* (發), translated here as springing up, literally shows a force penetrating through the crust of the earth, just as plants send up shoots in the spring which are capable of forcing their way through concrete and asphalt. And whereas the advice for winter is to retain warmth and preserve strength, the advice for the springtime is to stretch and move, maintaining the 'drive of life'. A little later in the text it says:

'To go against the *qi* of spring injures the liver (*gan* 肝)…'

In classical Chinese medicine, the liver *qi* is seen to be firm, strong and forceful, but very flexible; it moves and stimulates. It spreads its influence through the body in its capacity to 'master free-flow'. It allows ease of movement and exchange. Any blockage to this movement of free-flow, physically, mentally or emotionally, will damage the liver *qi*.

As the kidney *qi* governs the seeding and germination of life, the liver *qi* represents birth and the initial impetus of growth. And as the springing up and spreading out of spring is dependent on the storage and preservation of the winter, so the dynamic strength of the liver *qi* must be rooted in the kidneys.

The resonances of wood and the liver are seen in Suwen chapter 5:

---

33 The Way of Heaven, p. 107, The Liver, Monkey Press 1994, p.10

'The eastern quarter produces wind
wind produces wood
wood produces the sour taste
the sour taste produces the liver
the liver produces muscular strength.'[34]

Wood is related to the wind, to the stirring of things into life and motion; it is similar to the effects of the *yang qi*. Within medicine, wind may act as an external force, driving the other climates of cold, heat, dampness and dryness into the body; while within the body, wind defines symptoms which move around, come and go, sometimes creating irritability or itching.

Wood is also related here to the sour taste. The taste of a food reflects its active chemical constituents, and the sour taste, though contractive, stimulates movement and activity within the digestive system. Small amounts of the sour taste stimulate the liver, though too much can cause damage. The sour taste resonates with the liver and therefore helps to build and maintain the liver *qi*.

Muscular strength

The relationship between wood and muscular movement (*jin* 筋) suggests an association with the physical nature of muscular tissue, which resembles the fibrous structure of plants, but also the control of bodily movement. The character is made with the bamboo radical at the top, the part of the body (肉/月) and strength (力). This is not so much the bulk of the muscle, which is usually related to the flesh, and therefore the

---

34 The Liver, p. 44; The Rhythm at the Heart of the World, p. 29

earth element, but the ability to move; it is the flexability and strength, the contraction and expansion of the muscle fibres that allow physical movement. Suwen chapter 2 advises that in the springtime we 'pace the courtyard in great strides' – suggesting the benefit of physical movement after the hibernation of the winter months. The ability to bend and stretch, to be straight and flexible – are qualities attributed to wood, and in the human body, this is the effect of the liver *qi*. In order to provide free-flow of blood and *qi*, the body needs to be supple; areas of tightness and tension leading to stagnation and blockage.

Blockages within the liver *qi* may cause symptoms of shaking and trembling, violent spasms or cramps, muscle contractions or weakness. The health and strength of muscular activity depends on both the *qi* and the blood of the liver. Liver blood is necessary for the correct lubrication of the tendons and both the irrigation and nutrition of the muscle fibres. This lack of irrigation can lead to symptoms such as shaking and trembling, or cramps – whereas an over-powerful rising up of liver *qi* may cause seizures. It is always the balance of *yin* and *yang*, *qi* and blood within each organ system that is crucial to its good functioning.

The classical texts also mention an aspect of the muscular force called *zong jin* (宗 筋). We have seen the character *zong* (宗) in relation to the *zong qi* (宗 氣) which gathers in the chest, and gave it the possible name of 'ancestral'. *Zong jin* may be translated as the ancestral muscle, or the gathering of the muscles, and is located in the perineum; it forms the basic core strength which holds the organs in place, preventing prolapse. It controls the erection in men and the position and flexibility of the uterus in women. It binds around the lower orifices and anchors the base of the spine – providing strength and flexibility to the spinal chord. The character *zong* (宗) is used here to convey a connection to the basic power of life, through the power of the erection and the ability to hold and maintain a pregnancy, as well as its fundamental role in creating deep coherence within the body organs and the maintenance of function through the flexibility of the spine with its nervous system functions. The body has three of these gatherings; the *zong qi* which accumulates in the chest, the *zong jin* which gathers the muscular strength in the perineum, and the *zong mai*, a gathering of the meridian network around the eyes, creating a connection with the brain. The liver meridian flows in this area and its muscular meridian binds around the perineum and the base of the penis.

In the description of the cycles of fertility for men in Suwen chapter 1, the liver is mentioned in association with the muscles:

> 'At seven times eight years, the liver *qi* declines; the muscles no longer move.'[35]

This may refer to general muscular movement, but many commentators suggest that as this text is specifically referring to fertility, the inability to sustain an erection is also suggested here. In Suwen chapter 2 we read that to go against the *qi* of winter:

> '...will cause impotence (*wei* 痿) and deficiency in the spring, through an insufficient supply to the production of life.'[36]

Impotence (*wei* 痿) refers to any kind of muscular weakness and flaccidity, but in particular sexual impotence. Spring is associated with fertility, with the arousing of life force, but this is dependent on the

---

35 The Way of Heaven, p. 83

36 ibid. p. 121

ability of the kidneys to store and maintain. The liver blood must be nourished by the *yin* of the kidneys, which provide the firm basis for the spreading up and moving outwards of the liver *qi*. The liver is the wood, but the kidneys provide the strong roots for all its activity and growth.

As the strength of the kidney *qi* is seen externally in the hair and teeth, that of the liver is seen in the quality of the nails. The same quality of *qi* which gives the tendino-muscular strength within the body manifests itself externally in the nails. It is also suggested that the nails are an extension of the tendons. The same quality of firmness and suppleness used to define wood also applies to the quality of the nails. If the liver *qi* is weak they may be too soft, if the liver *qi* is too strong and lacking in good nourishment from the blood, the nails may be fibrous, ridged and brittle. These associations are also found in Suwen chapter 9:

> 'The liver… its flourishing aspect is in the nails
> its full power is in muscular force
> its function is to produce blood and *qi*.'[37]

And in Suwen chapter 10:

> 'When a human being is at rest, the blood returns to the liver.
> When the liver receives the blood, one can see clearly,
> the feet receive blood and one can walk,
> the palms of the hands receive blood and one can grasp things,
> the fingers receive blood and one can pick up small things…'[38]

---

37 The Liver, p. 62

38 ibid. p. 79

The text of Suwen chapter 10 suggests that not only the larger actions of physical movement are controlled by the liver and dependent on the ability of the liver to store and circulate the blood, but small movements of proprioception, co-ordination of hand and eye, muscle and brain are also dependent on a supply of blood and *qi* from the liver.

Colours, sounds, emotions

Returning to Suwen chapter 5:

'…of parts of the body it is the muscular forces (*jin* 筋)
of the *zang* it is the liver
of colours it is azure green (*cang* 蒼),
of notes it is *jue*,
of noises it is to shout,
of reactive movements it is to grasp (*wo* 握)
of the orifices it is the eye…'[39]

The colour associated with liver wood and spring (*cang* 蒼) is translated here as azure green. It is the colour of new life in the springtime. In chapter 4 the wood element and the liver are associated with the character *qing* (青), which is the colour of life, and is often used to describe something that is full of vital essences.

Jue is the third note of the pentatonic scale, a note which in the Book of Rites is said to 'resonate with the people'. To shout is the human expression of a forceful outward movement of *qi* expressed through the voice. In martial arts the shout is used to propel the *qi* and to assist and

---

39 ibid. p. 44

direct physical movement. In the same way that continual sighing may show an imbalance within the kidney *qi*, so a loud shouting voice suggests an over-aggressive liver *qi*. Alcohol stimulates the liver, and its effect on the liver *qi* is heard as voices are raised. But if the liver *qi* is suppressed, a loud expelling of air will be beneficial. Many of the *qi gong* exercises to stimulate the liver *qi* include the use of sound with a strong exhalation.

The bodily reaction is to grasp (*wo* 握) which is specifically grasping something with the hand, but which can also be seen as a general tensing of the muscles.

The connection of sight with the liver function is as important and complex as that of muscular movement. It is an intrinsic part of the classical Chinese understanding of the liver *qi*, and provides an interesting example of the interdependence of mind/body, physical, mental, emotional and what may be called the spiritual aspects of the human being.

The upper orifices are vital organs for the reception of information from the environment. Each orifice functions in a different way, and is categorized according to its five element resonance. In the case of the eyes, their association with wood and the liver suggests a clarity of vision, a far-sightedness which enables one to assess a situation take the correct action. The quality of the liver *qi*, which reflects the *qi* of the springtime, is to spread and move and to project, and this association with sight reflects this ability to project and to grasp, both mentally and physically. Clarity of mind, the ability to make a quick decision, to respond appropriately to information gained, all come under the authority of the liver, which is said in Suwen chapter 8 to give the ability to 'assess circumstances and to make plans'.[40]

---

40 The Secret Treatise of the Spiritual Orchid, Monkey Press 2003, p. 58

A liver pathology may be suspected when the eyes do not see clearly, if the vision is blurred, or the eyes have difficulty in focusing. But there is also an involvement with the *qi* of the liver if there is an inability to make decisions, to assess and move forward. A kind of 'stuckness' in life may be seen as an expression of a blockage of the *qi* of the liver and of its *yang* counterpart the gallbladder.

This kind of inner vision suggests a link with the imagination, and Suwen chapter 9 says that:

'The liver …is the residence of the *hun*…'[41]

We will look more closely at this concept when we discuss the five spiritual aspects (*wu shen* 五 神) – but it is interesting to note here that the *hun* (魂), often translated as the ethereal soul, is related to dreams, imagination, visions, and what might be called 'remote viewing'. In Lingshu chapter 8 the *hun* are said to come and go with the *shen*,[42] they are that aspect of dreams and imagination that can travel, and in some daoist visualization and meditation techniques, the *hun* are said to travel to different places. Here we are more concerned with the notion that the liver and the orifice of the eyes have a connection within the classical literature to this idea of second sight. Some individuals may be more attuned to remember or to capture information, just as some of us retain and capture our dreams, but the *hun* comes and goes, following the *shen*, whether we remember its journeys or not. Bringing our attention to a particular facility often means that it will become more apparent to us. In Chinese medical terms, this is simply an extension of the function of

---

41 The Liver, p. 62

42 The Heart in Lingshu chapter 8, Monkey Press 2004, p. 51

the liver *qi* in its capacity to govern free-flow.

We read in chapter 8 of the Lingshu that the liver blood is the container for the *hun*. In the constant interweaving and blending between *yin yang*, blood and *qi*, the *yang* quality of the *hun* needs a substantial basis within the body if it is not to constantly float away. Dreams and visions may be seen as an expression of liver pathology, especially if the patient shows other signs of being ungrounded and not able to deal with the realities of life. There may be a tendency to live in the imagination and float away, while being unable to make practical decisions.

The *yin* ability of the liver blood to collect, to be renewed and clarified and act as a basis for both the liver *qi* and the *hun*, is dependent on the water of the kidneys. This relationship is at the basis of five phase interactions within the internal organs and their functions. This section of Suwen chapter 5 on the resonances of wood and the liver concludes:

'…of the emotions it is anger.'

Anger is simply an expression of *qi*. As the shout is an outward movement of the voice, anger is a movement upwards and outwards, often quite violent, of the *qi*. Shouting and other expressions of anger – which may also involve grasping or hitting – are a good example of how the *qi* of one person may effect another. We all know what it feels like to be around someone who is angry. We even feel their suppressed anger – and clinically this is often what we are dealing with in liver pathology. Both are an interruption to the natural free-flow of *qi*, and therefore damage the liver and all its associated functions.

The free-flow of liver *qi* and the ability of the liver to store and release blood governs the cycles of menstruation, and the emotions which often accompany the menstrual cycle may be seen as a lack of balance within the *qi* and blood of the liver. The ability of the uterus to hold and store and also to release blood may be affected by blockage to the liver *qi*, and the kind of symptoms frequently seen in pre-menstrual tension are typical of liver pathology. There may be anger or irritability, which has no real external cause, but is simply an expression of a blockage of the liver *qi*. There may also be bloating and pain, distension in the sides of the trunk, swelling of the breasts, which are all symptoms of blockage in the free-flow of liver *qi*. The flow of blood during menstruation may also reflect the liver's ability to hold and to release. Intermittent flow, a kind of stopping and starting of the menstruation, is one common pattern. The liver *qi* also affects the regularity of the menstrual cycle.

The text of Suwen chapter 4 presents similar correspondences, but not quite the same as those of chapter 5, suggesting that at this time several slightly differing versions of five element correspondences existed. Even in Suwen chapter 5, this part of the text appears to be a compilation from several earlier sources.[43] In the classical texts, these resonances were never seen as the kind of clearly defined lists and tables we may see in text books today, but as examples of possible correspondence within a specific vibration of *qi* patterning.

> 'The natural green colour of the eastern quarter
> penetrates and spreads to the liver.
> It opens at the orifice of the eye,
> it stores its essences in the liver.
> Its disturbance is seen in trembling and shaking…its illness is seen in the muscular forces.'[44]

---

43 Wu Xing: The Five Elements in Classical Chinese Texts, p. 87
44 Suwen chapter 4 in The Liver, p. 21

FIRE AND THE HEART

The text of the Hongfan tells us that 'fire ascends and burns', and within the various aspects of the fire element within Chinese medicine it is the tempering of this fire that is vital to life. Life requires the correct sustaining warmth; too much heat is destructive, insufficient heat and the various transformation processes occurring within the body will then become sluggish and ineffective. This is often illustrated in the old alchemical texts by a cauldron, which must have the correct strength of fire below it, the correct amount of water within it to create a good mixture of *yin* and *yang*, *qi* and blood, and to provide the correct environment to contain and sustain the essences and spirits (*jing shen* 精 神).

Fire is related to the summer, to heat, to the south and to the maximum expression of *yang*. The young *yang* movement of the *qi* in springtime grows and comes to fruition in the summer months. The summer solstice is the time of maximum light – when the warmth of the sun allows crops to ripen and all kinds of plants to flower and set fruit. In Suwen chapter 2 it says:

'The three months of summer are called prospering and developing the flower. The *qi* of heaven and earth intertwine and the ten thousand beings flower and bring forth fruit.'[45]

The dynamic movement of the spring gives way to an opening out, a

---

45 The Way of Heaven, p. 111

flourishing, which is characteristic of the fire element. The text goes on to advise that we assist the *qi*, which naturally flows to the surface, fulfilling the beauty and strength of life:

> 'This corresponds to the *qi* of summer, which maintains the growth of life. To go against this would injure the *qi* of the heart (*xin* 心).'

As the spring matures into summer, the dynamism of the liver gives way to the gentle opening of the heart. Midsummer has a certain stillness, it represents the time of fruition, a pause, before the *yang* begins its decline. The heart reflects this stillness, and an openness to spirit which is often celebrated in the festivals of midsummer. Suwen chapter 5 gives the five phase resonances of fire and the heart:

> 'The southern quarter produces heat
> Heat produces fire, fire produces bitter
> Bitter produces the heart (*xin* 心)
> The heart produces blood (*xue* 血)...
> In heaven it is heat, on earth it is fire
> Of parts of the body, it is the vital circulation (*mai* 脈)
> Of the *zang* organs, it is the heart
> Of colours it is red.'[46]

The blood and its circulation

The heart and the fire element control the blood (*xue* 血) and its circulation (*mai* 脈). *Mai* refers both to the blood vessels and to the

---

46 The Ryhthm at the Heart of the World, p. 33

circulation of the blood within the vessels. It is also the pulse, where the vital circulation of the blood can be felt. The red colour of the blood distinguishes it from all other body fluids and signifies the stamp of the heart, which holds the position of emperor in the hierarchy of the organs. In order for the blood to circulate well, the heart must be clear and free of obstruction; unlike the other *zang*, which store essences, the heart circulates the blood – but it also stores the spirits, as we see in Suwen chapter 23:

> 'The heart stores (*cang* 藏) the spirits (*shen* 神)'

And also in Lingshu chapter 8:

> 'The heart stores (*cang* 藏) the *mai* (脈); the *mai* are the dwelling place of the spirits (*shen* 神).'

Here the spirits are said to dwell in the *mai* (脈), which in turn are stored, or treasured and maintained, by the heart. The *mai* is the vital network for the circulation of the blood, and the red colour is also an indication of the presence of the spirits within the blood. The presence of the spirits implies an intelligence; the blood carries information and allows sensation and perception. It literally brings life and consciousness to the body. The character *xin* (心) has the meaning of heart and mind in classical texts, and often may be translated as heart/mind to remind us of this. The heart is the home of the spirits, and welcomes the spirits – attracting them by providing suitable conditions for their sustenance. The spirits like a calm heart/mind; the correct richness of the blood; a regularity of movement through the *mai*.

Many of the old daoist texts liken the spirits to birds – if they have the right conditions they will settle, and even build nests, but if there is too much agitation, they just fly away. What disturbs the heart most is the emotions. And the free-flow of *qi* through the heart may be disturbed by each of the different emotional states in a different way.

Sounds and emotions
Suwen chapter 5 continues:

'Of musical tones it is *zhi*
Of sounds it is laughter (*xiao* 笑)
Of reaction to change, it is oppression (*you* 憂)...
Of expressions of will, it is elation (*xi* 喜)...'

The tone *zhi* is said to bring harmony, even to create joy.[47] In the same way laughter, when appropriate, loosens the *qi* and smoothes the circulation, though in excess it may create agitation. The character *you* (憂), oppression, literally suggests a pressure on the heart, a kind of oppressive grief which stops the flow of *qi* in the chest, preventing the flourishing of life that the fire element strives for. Elation (*xi* 喜) elevates the *qi* – it opens upwards and spreads out. But as with laughter, it may go too far and become a kind of floaty spaced-out, ungrounded state, or equally an overexcitement. The natural joy of being alive is appropriate to the heart – and gives the spirits the most attractive kind of nest.

The bitter taste is associated with the heart, and it tends to have a draining, clearing and sometimes purging effect. Salty and bitter tastes may be used to regulate the relationship between heart and kidneys.

---

47 The Rhythm at the Heart of the World, p. 93

The tongue

Each organ is associated with an orifice in Suwen chapter 5, but the heart is said to 'master the tongue (*xin zhu she* 心 主 舌)'. Not usually considered as an orifice, the tongue nevertheless is a means of outward expression – particularly in its relation to speech. And the heart is said to bring discrimination to the speech. Wild, erratic, nonsensical speech is a sign that the heart/mind is disturbed; measured, thoughtful speech a sign of good communication with the heart and the spirits. But we also find in Lingshu chapter 17:

> 'The *qi* of the heart communes with the tongue. When the heart is in harmony, the tongue can recognize the five tastes.'[48]

In Suwen chapter 4, however, we see that the heart is related to the ears. In this chapter, the kidneys are related to the lower orifices, and the ears are therefore free for association with the heart.

> 'The red colour of the southern quarter communes with the heart; it opens its orifice at the ears.'

The double aspect of the heart

The fire element has two aspects, which reflect the radiance and life-giving energy of the sun and the fire that is within the earth. Within the human body these two aspects are referred to as sovereign fire (*jun huo* 君 火) and minister fire (*xiang huo* 相 火). Sovereign fire refers to the light and clarity of the heart/mind, and its ability to store the spirits

---

48 The Double Aspect of the Heart, Monkey Press 2012, p. 33

(*shen* 神); minister fire refers to the heart in its active role of mastering the blood and the circulation and its relationship with the fire of *ming men* (命 門), the gate of life. The fire of *ming men* in the lower abdomen provides the warmth and stimulation for all transformation while assuring the continuation of the original patterning. Sovereign fire and minister fire constantly resonate and interact within human physiology and psychology; and the heart itself constantly reflects these two aspects, most apparently within its two meridians.

The kidneys are described as a double organ, there are two kidneys and they contain both *yin* and *yang*, fire and water. It is made clear in the text of the Nanjing that when six *zang* organs are mentioned, it is this double, *yin/yang*, nature of the kidneys that is referred to and not the double aspect of the heart.[49] This is despite the fact that the heart is represented by two meridians, while the kidneys only have one. There is only one heart, and its so-called double aspect refers to the heart in its two functions – that of a void and empty space for the reception of the spirits, and that of its mastery of the blood and its circulation. The heart in this capacity of mastery is the *xin zhu* (心 主), literally heart-mastering, a term that is seen frequently in expressions such as *xin zhu xue* (心 主 血), the heart masters the blood, and *xin zhu xue mai* (心 主 血 脈) the heart masters the blood circulation. What is referred to in modern books as the pericardium channel is, in the Chinese, the *xin zhu* – the heart as master, or the heart in its mastering capacity – the hand *jue yin*, and it is this channel which is mentioned in many of the classical texts as the channel most commonly used in treatment of heart pathology. In Suwen chapter 71, the Yellow Emperor asks why the heart meridian (hand *shao yin*) has no *shu* points (the five command or element points), and is told by his physician that the correct channel to

---

49 Nanjing difficulty 36 in The Kidneys

use is the *xin zhu*, although one may treat the heart meridian at the point Shenmen (Ht 7). In the Jiayijing, most points on the heart channel (*shao yin*) have no clinical indications.⁵⁰

The so-called pericardium channel (*xin zhu* 心 主) is related to the heart in its active role, and in its role of mastering the blood and circulation in particular. The heart channel itself, hand *shao yin*, is used here for calming the heart/mind and attracting the spirits. It is also interesting that in the more recently discovered Mawangdui texts, excavated from a tomb dating back to the 2nd century BCE, only one heart channel is mentioned – it is given the name heart (*xin* 心) but the described pathway resembles that of the modern pericardium channel.

But we are told in the text of the Taisu that the *xin zhu* meridian is governed by the *xin bao* (心 包) – the protection of the heart, which brings us closer to the pericardium designation.⁵¹ The aspect of the heart described as the *xin bao luo* (心 包 絡) may have a closer relationship to the Western concept of the pericardium, though the term conveys too material a meaning. *Xin* (心) is the heart, *bao* (包) is the protection around the heart, *luo* (絡) is the connecting network around the heart. *Bao* is a protective sac, and is most frequently seen in connection with the uterus, though it is also used to describe the intimate envelopes (*bao zhong* 包 中) in the depths of the belly from where life proceeds and grows. We can see here that this double aspect, double functioning, cannot be designated to one function or another – but is to be found in all aspects of the heart. With the *xin bao luo* there is the more material protective function of the *bao*, and also the connective, informational aspect of the *luo*.

This brings us back to the two aspects of the fire element designated

---

50 The Double Aspect of the Heart, p 55

51 ibid. p. 51

as sovereign and minister fire. Minister fire refers to the active function of the heart as *xin zhu* and *xin bao luo*, sovereign fire to the heart as emperor, seat of the mind and emotions and residence of the spirits. The *xin zhu* meridian is related to that of the triple heater in a *yin/yang*, internal/external relationship, and in Nanjing difficulty 25 we see:

> 'The *xin zhu* (heart as master) and the *san jiao* (triple heater) are related internally/externally (*biao/li*). These two have a name but no form (*wu xing* 無形).'[52]

So this second aspect the of the heart is described as having 'no form', and could therefore be seen as the heart in its functional role. But within this, and other texts of the Nanjing, 'no form' is also a reference to the closeness of this aspect of fire to the origins of life and to the function of fire in its transformative role. Some later commentators suggest that *wu xing* (無形) may also be translated as having no specific shape, and that both the *xin zhu* and the *san jiao* are not formed as other organs but imply a kind of shapeless, formless tissue which surrounds the organs. We will look at this again in association with the triple heater.

The two aspects of the fire element may also be seen as warmth and light – the gentle warmth, that is necessary for the maintenance of life and all its transformation processes, and the light and clarity of the mind and consciousness, which is also the consciousness within the body, a kind of body-knowing, as well as mental intelligence. The spirits of the heart, through its various connections (*luo* 絡), gather information from the upper orifices – the eyes and ears in particular – and use that information to direct the *qi* and blood.

---

52 Heart Master Triple Heater, p. 34

It is interesting to note that in modern Chinese dictionaries, the character *shen* (神) is found in various aspects of the nervous system, and '*shen* disorders' are likely to be disorders of the nervous system. The nerves themselves are called *shen jing* (神 經), pathways of the *shen*. It is the role of the heart/mind in maintaining a calm nervous system, in receiving the appropriate information from the senses via the sensory nerves, and reacting appropriately to that stimulation, that best describes the heart/*shen* relationship in modern terminology. The way that we react to various kinds of external stimulation, sight, sound, touch, taste, smell, either puts the heart at ease or creates agitation within the system. Many of the classical philosophical texts suggest that in order to 'nourish the heart' we should learn not to be reactive, but respond in a natural way – with neither like or dislike, preference or pre-conceived ideas. It says in the Guanzi Neiye:

'When our hearts are well-regulated, our senses are well-regulated too.'[53]

The central palace

Suwen chapter 8 designates a function to each of the twelve *zang fu*, and it says of the heart:

'The heart is the master and sovereign; the light of the spirits stem from it.'[54]

But later in the chapter, after defining the charges of the lung, the liver and the gallbladder, we come across the term *tan zhong* (or *dan zhong* 膻 中):

---

53 Guanzi Neiye, XIV 10

54 Suwen chapter 8 in The Secret Treatise of the Spiritual Orchid, p. 36

'*Tan zhong* has the charge of resident and envoy; elation and joy stem from it.⁵⁵'

Tan zhong is the name given to the centre of the chest, the place where the *zong qi* gathers, before beginning its circulation within the meridian system. It is the central palace – the sea of *qi* in the chest, and it gives the regular beat to the heart and rhythm to the lungs. The concept of 'resident and envoy' is similar to that of *xin bao luo* – in its function of protection of the emperor, and connection via the *mai* to the periphery. Elation and joy, the emotions generally associated with the heart itself, are here associated with this central palace, this pooling of *qi* at the centre of the chest.

'*Tan zhong* is at the origin of the circulation of *qi* and the movement of blood…'⁵⁶

Chapter 8 of the Suwen is so dense in information and profound in meaning, that it is given the title 'Secret Treatise of the Spiritual Orchid'. It is a treatise of such importance that it is stored in the library of the emperor which is called the Spiritual Orchid. And here this second aspect of the heart is given the name *tan zhong*.

Tan (膻) is very close to the character *tan* (壇) which is used to describe the Temple of Heaven (*tian tan* 天 壇) in the Imperial Palace. In this case the character has the radical for the earth (土) rather than the radical for the part of the body (肉/月). Claude Larre suggests that this palace at the centre of the chest is a temple within the body for the

---

55 ibid. p. 90
56 ibid. p. 101

reception and distribution of the influences of heaven, just as the Temple of Heaven fulfils this function within the Imperial Palace.[57] *Tan zhong* acts as a palace for the collection and distribution of *qi*; it receives influences from the spirits and distributes them in the form of elation and joy.

This is the foundation of the ability of the heart to bring discrimination to the five senses via the orifices. In discriminating between what is appropriate and inappropriate within the tastes, for example, the heart assures good health through correct diet. If the heart is in tune, and free from desires, it will not crave what is unhealthy, but appreciate simply what is nourishing and beneficial.

Many of the pathologies associated with the heart, reflect an agitation of the mind and disquiet of the *shen*. This may manifest as unrest, insomnia, palpitations; excess sweating, a red complexion. Suwen chapter 9 gives a concise summary of the heart and its attributes:

> 'The heart is the root of life,
> Its fluctuations are controlled by the spirits.
> Its flourishing aspect is in the complexion,
> Its full power is in the vital circulation (*mai* 脈);
> It is the great *yang* within the *yang*
> It communicates with the *qi* of summer.'

Although the heart is a *zang* organ, it is also the *yang* within the *yang*; the great illuminator, the sun within the sky. As the kidneys were related to the origins of life, all that we inherit and pass on, the heart reflects what we aspire to – our capacity for illumination and alignment with our original nature (*xing* 性).

---

57 ibid, p. 95-97

EARTH – SPLEEN AND STOMACH

The Hongfan tells us that 'the earth receives seeds and gives crops' – a simple phrase which contains the essence of the earth element. How does the seed within the earth germinate and grow? How does the human body take in food and transform that food into flesh and blood? This is the mystery of the earth, and of the function of the spleen and stomach within Chinese medicine.

Earth governs the central region, and enables distribution and transformation (*yun hua* 運化). But the earth is not associated with one of the four seasons and therefore is not mentioned in Suwen chapter 2. We are given no indication for the action of the spleen by understanding its position within the ordering and successions of the four seasons. Suwen chapter 9, which describes each of the *zang* organs as being 'in resonance with the *qi*' of a particular season, describes the spleen as being 'in resonance with the earth'. But the earth, in the traditional Chinese calendar, governs the two week period between the seasons – it governs the transition from one season to another, and in its position at the centre, rotates and harmonizes the *qi* of the four seasons like the hub of a wheel, allowing winter a proper succession to spring; summer the correct and balanced shift into autumn. The *qi* of the earth balances and harmonizes the *qi* of the other four elements, and the *qi* of the spleen and stomach harmonizes and balances the *qi* of the *zang*.

Suwen chapter 5:

> 'The central region produces dampness
> Dampness produces the earth
> The earth produces the sweet
> The sweet produces the spleen (*pi* 脾)
> The spleen produces flesh…'[58]

In the many descriptions of geographic location made around this time, the central region is one of fertility, of the best crops, the most refined and beautiful people – and China has always been known as the central kingdom. Whereas other regions have too much cold or heat or wind or dryness – too many mountains or forests, deserts and seas, the central region has the correct balance of fire and water, sun and rain, to combine to make the earth fertile and produce the sweet taste of grains and vegetables. These in turn nourish the spleen and stomach which enable the grains and other foods to be broken down, absorbed and distributed for the building and rebuilding (*ying* 營) of the body.

The spleen and stomach (*pi wei* 脾 胃) control the digestive process – allowing grains and vegetables to be incorporated. The ability of the human body to transform a carrot – or any other form of sustenance – into its own flesh and blood, reflects the state of the spleen *qi*. Are we good at absorbing nutrients, or does food pass through too quickly? Or is the digestion sluggish, in which case we are more likely to gain extra

---

58 The Rhythm at the Heart of the World, p. 35

pounds rather than extract energy from food. The earth element reflects this ability to absorb and transform and therefore it controls the shape of the body, the quality of the flesh, the ability to absorb nourishment and eliminate waste in an appropriate way.

Dampness is the climate related to the earth, and the fertility of the soil requires the correct balance of fire and water to give the best conditions for seeds to mature, plants to grow, give fruit, and set seed again. Too dry and the soil will be subject to wind erosion, too wet and it will be waterlogged, with no air within its structure. No sun and there will be no ripening. The earth element holds the place of balance between fire and water and the example of making pottery is often used to illustrate this. The clay must have the right amount of moisture to allow it to be shaped; the kiln the correct temperature for the firing. Within the body, dampness shows a lack of fluid transformation (which is the action of fire upon water) causing stagnation and blockage. Suwen chapter 5 continues:

> 'Of colours it is yellow
> Of musical notes it is *gong*
> Of sounds it is singing…
> Of reactions to change it is belching
> Of orifices it is the mouth
> Of tastes it is sweet
> Of expressions of will, it is thought (*si* 思)…'[59]

Everything about the centre and the earth is harmonious. Its colour is the yellow of fertile soil or ripe grain; its note brings harmony, its

---

59 ibid.

sound is singing, its reactive movement to belch or burp. The mouth has a clear relationship with the digestive system, and the shape, size, colour, particularly of the lips, are used to define various strengths and deficiencies in the spleen *qi*. The sweet taste blends and harmonizes the others and makes them more easily digestible. A herbal formula will often contain a sweet herb such as liquorice to blend the other herbs and assure assimilation.

Thought

But then we come to its 'expression of will' – so why are the spleen and the earth connected with thought? And is thought an emotion? A clue to the meaning of this association comes from Suwen chapter 39, where we read that:

'When there is obsessive thought (*si* 思) the *qi* is knotted.'[60]

Thinking is a process of turning things around in the mind, and this emotional state associated with the spleen and the earth element is often referred to as over-thinking, obsessive thought, worry and concern. But the Chinese character *si* (思) is simply thought, and is comprised of the ideograms of the brain and the heart. This aspect of human function acts as a kind of central go-between for the kidneys – governing the will and linked to the brain, and the heart – governing the spirit and the mind. Thinking comes about when these two are aligned and in balance and communicating one with the other. The central position and rotational action of the spleen *qi* allow the cogitation, the turning around in the

---

60 The Seven Emotions, p. 54

mind, the consideration that makes up the thinking process. But if we think too much, without maybe employing the directive decision making ability of the liver, the *qi* can become knotted. We can get caught up in things, stuck, entangled in the machinations of the mind.

Over-thinking also affects the digestive process – a literal knotting of the *qi* which interferes with the natural absorption and distribution of nutrients.

The five tastes
Suwen chapter 8, the Secret Treatise, tells us that:

> 'The spleen and stomach have the charge of storehouses and granaries (*cang lin* 倉 廩). The five tastes (*wu wei* 五 味) stem from them.'[61]

The Chinese characters translated as storehouses and granaries are *cang* (倉) and *lin* (廩), which have the slightly differing meanings of a place where food is received and temporarily stored, and the place from which it is distributed. The stomach is responsible for the reception, the spleen for the distribution. The five tastes (*wu wei* 五 味) represent all the different aspects of food, the chemical constituents which make a particular taste or flavour and create a specific resonance with a part of the body; the sour taste, for example, resonating with the liver *qi*; the bitter taste entering the heart and descending fire. The sweet taste resonates with the spleen, harmonizing the other tastes and allowing them to circulate well and to the correct place, so that the food that we eat becomes not only part of the physical body but also the *qi*.

---

61 The Secret Treatise of the Spiritual Orchid, p. 109

The function of the spleen is distribution (*yun* 運) and transformation (*hua* 化). The character *yun* contains the idea of rotation, providing an even distribution of influences – in the way that rain may fall from heaven. *Hua* suggests the natural transformations of the life process. The spleen is responsible in this way for the more subtle aspects of the digestive process, the stomach and the other organs of transport along the digestive tract, for the more gross.

'The spleen is the messenger (*shi* 使), the stomach is the market (*shi* 市).'[62]

The spleen receives the most subtle essences of food as 'the five tastes' and distributes to each of the five *zang* appropriately. This subtle *qi* acquired from food is *ying qi* (營 氣), usually translated as nutritive *qi*, but the character also contains the meaning of constructing and rebuilding. It is the *qi* which is responsible for the constant rebuilding and renewal of tissues and cells.

This distribution of the *qi* of nourishment and rebuilding by the spleen controls the shape of the body, but also gives the body its strength. Though the ability to move is generally associated with the wood *qi* and the liver, the actual physical bulk of the muscles is controlled by the spleen, and without nourishment, the muscles will have no strength:

'When the *qi* of the spleen is empty, the four limbs cannot move.'[63]

The control of the four limbs, or the ability to move, is attributed to the nutritive function of the spleen, but in the same text it states:

---

62 Suwen chapter 52 in Spleen and Stomach, Monkey Press 2004, p. 100
63 Lingshu chapter 8 in Spleen and Stomach, p. 97

'The spleen stores the *ying* (營); the *ying* is the dwelling place of the *yi* (意).'[64]

The *yi* (意) is the aspect of spirit associated with the spleen and the earth and is generally translated as intent or purpose. Similarly in Suwen chapter 23:

'The spleen stores the *yi* (意)'.[65]

The nourishment of the spleen not reaching the four limbs creates a kind of paralysis, or inability to move, but this also suggests that the messages from the brain are unable to get through to the the appropriate receptors in the limbs – there is a breakdown in communication in the messaging system which prevents consciousness from directing *qi* to the limbs. We will look at the *yi* in more depth in the section on the aspects of spirit, but in this inability to move the four limbs, there is not only a suggestion of physical emaciation, but also the idea of a lack of the will to move, or the inability to execute the will to move – a split between the will and the action, which is the *yi*.

The spleen as centre

In its function as a centre within the body, the spleen is responsible for keeping things in their proper place. The central *qi* (*zhong qi* 中氣) holds the internal organs in position, and any kind of prolapse may be seen as an insufficiency of this central *qi* and by extension of the spleen *qi*.

---

64 ibid. p 97
65 ibid. p. 94

The spleen *qi* also holds the blood within the confines of the vessels, and haemorrhage or seepage into the tissues is also associated with a weakness of the spleen *qi*. This same lack of the holding function is also seen in other discharges and leakages, such as leucorrhea and seminal emissions. Both conditions may also have other causes, but spleen *qi* deficiency should always be considered where a lack of containment is present.

Late summer

Although the classical texts stress the importance of the spleen as holding the central position, and this is the most useful way to understand its function within classical Chinese medicine, when referring to the yearly cycle, the earth element may also be given a place between the summer and the autumn – that of late summer.

This suggests an association between the earth *qi* and the harvest and productivity of the earth, but it may also indicate that this particular interseasonal period – that of the return from full expansion of the *yang* to the beginning of the contraction of the *yin* – as the most difficult to navigate. The *qi*, which has become used to the pleasant expansive movement of the summer, may react to the retraction and constriction of the autumn. It may also be caught off guard when the *qi* of the seasons changes suddenly. Whereas nature responds naturally to a change in the *qi* pattern, the human psyche often goes against what is natural in an attempt to extend the pleasures of summer! In the same way, expansion and growth are the preferred patterns for society at large. There is a natural distancing from the necessity of restriction and control; but if this phase of the cycle is ignored, there will always be an eventual crash, as growth and expansion become unsustainable.

Placing the earth element between the summer and autumn corresponds to the pattern of the *sheng* (生) or generation cycle of the five elements, which is most commonly used to describe the pattern of five element interaction.

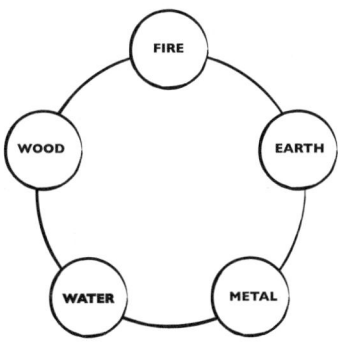

Fig 8: The generation (sheng 生) cycle of the five elements/phases

Post-heaven

We have seen that the *qi* of the kidneys, and its associated *yuan qi* (original *qi*) may be referred to as pre-heaven, or former heaven *qi*. This strange term is a translation of the Chinese *xian tian qi* (先 天 氣), and it suggests the original *qi* which is inherited at birth. Post-heaven, or *hou tian qi* (後 天 氣) is associated with the spleen and stomach, and describes the interaction of the pre-heaven, inherited or constitutional *qi*, with food and air. In the womb, the foetus is nourished by the *qi* and blood of the mother, and develops its own original *qi*. At birth, the first intake of the breath and suckle of the breast begins the individual process of energy production – the original *qi* acting as a kind of catalyst in the process of cellular respiration.

Pre- and post-heaven *qi* are terms not found in the Neijing – but this distinction helps to clarify the innate differences in function of the kidneys and the spleen. According to Elisabeth Rochat de la Vallée:

> 'The essences of pre-heaven are not merely essences present at the moment of conception. They are the inborn mechanism and structure for the rebuilding and reconstitution of the body on the model of the first composition of mother/father, *yin/yang*, fire/water. The kidneys are the guarantee of this, and this function is the meaning of the essences of the kidneys.'[66]

The spleen and stomach, as post-heaven *qi*, receive instruction from the kidneys. Their position at the centre and as the earth element (*tu* 土) allows exchange and movement between heaven (*tian* 天) and earth (*di* 地) – ascending and descending, diffusing and concentrating, separating clear and unclear. The spleen therefore acts as a centre for all nutrition, which includes providing a basis for the production of blood.

---

66 Spleen and Stomach, p. 88

METAL AND THE LUNG

Metal is the most dense and contracted of substances, and yet we read in the Hongfan that 'metal yields and changes'. Wood and metal have both *yin* and *yang* qualities, reflecting the nature of the *qi* in spring and autumn. Wood bends and can also be straight, metal has strength and rigidity, and yet it can also be melted and re-smelted. Metal is the most mutable as well as the most dense and solid material. Wood may both bend and be straight, but once a tree is cut and carved to make a seat, it cannot become a tree again. Metal however, can be forged and reforged – made into a cooking pot or a temple bell, and then melted down to make a sword or a shield in times of war; melted again and reforged in times of peace. In the same way that scrap metal was collected up to be used in the war efforts of 20th century Europe – so the people of ancient China would give up their bells and cauldrons in time of war for the forging of weapons. So despite being the strongest and most rigid of substances, metal can change its shape. In its rigidity it is strangely adaptable.

Autumn and the metal element are often symbolized by the scales – everything has to be weighed up, judged, and all that is deemed unnecessary for the continuity of life throughout the winter months is discarded, in order to maintain life in the correct balance. The autumn is also the turning point, where the richness and abundance of harvest, moves into storing and preparing for the lean winter months.

Autumn is the beginning of the contraction of the *qi*, the beginning of the *yin* movement inwards and downwards. This is a natural and unavoidable reaction to a change of temperature and light. Leaves fall from the trees, some mammals begin to prepare for hibernation. This is not a conscious decision, but simply part of a natural cycle. Warmth stimulates circulation, cold slows down. The sap withdraws into the depths of the tree, and is no longer able to sustain nourishment of its peripheral twigs and leaves; the blood and *qi* of the bear slows down, he feels sluggish, finds shelter and goes to sleep. Autumn and the metal element are the preparation for the separation of the winter, when *yin* and *yang* turn their backs on each other and no longer communicate.

We read in Suwen chapter 2:

> 'The three months of autumn are called plentiful and balancing (*ping* 平) The *qi* of heaven becomes pressing. The *qi* of earth is resplendent.'[67]

The resplendence and plenitude are related to the early stages of the autumn, the late summer, the time of harvest and gathering in. But in order to gather the crops they must be cut. And after the abundance and free-flow of *qi* in the summer, autumn is the time to take stock, balance things up, store what we need and let go of what is no longer necessary to get through the winter. The Chinese character here translated as balance is *ping* (平), which has a beautiful resemblance to the scales. In Han dynasty China, autumn was also the time of punishments, of judgement and taking matters to court. This concept of the balance and of judgement is also seen in the astrological sign of Libra, the scales, which is the zodiac sign related to mid-autumn. The pressure of the *qi* of heaven at this time

---

67 The Way of Heaven, p. 115

reflects the idea of contraction and restriction.

> 'Exerting the will peacefully and calmly
> To soften the repressive effects of autumn…
> Clarifying and freshening the lung *qi*
> Which corresponds with the *qi* of the autumn.
> This is the way to maintain the harvesting of life.'[68]

This part of the chapter ends with the statement, 'To go against the natural movement of *qi* in the autumn will injure the lung (*fei* 肺)'. The expansion of the wood and liver *qi*, associated with the spring, is rooted in the water of the kidneys – and here in the autumn we have the opposite movement. The autumn begins within the full expansion of the summer, and presses down towards the winter. In the same way, the lungs inhale the *qi* in their expansion, and press down into the lower body with the exhalation. The double movement of the lungs is seen in their ability to descend the *qi* to the kidneys, and also to diffuse clear and fresh *qi* to the surface of the skin.

Suwen chapter 5:

> 'The western quarter produces dryness
> Dryness produces metal
> Metal produces the pungent taste
> The pungent taste produces the lung
> The lungs produce the skin and body hair.'[69]

---

68 ibid.
69 The Lung, p. 17

Western China is a land of mountains and deserts. But it is also the direction of the setting sun. Unlike the east and the dawn, when everything is stirred into to life, the setting sun is a time of calm and quiet. Three of the 14 day periods in the autumn are called white dew, cold dew and white frost, and illustrate both the association with the white colour, but also the way in which this pressure of the *qi* of heaven forces liquids out onto the surface of the earth, which freeze or evaporate, creating dryness within the soil. This is a time of sudden cold and the condensation of vapours, and the cycle of evaporation and condensation which is seen in nature is reflected in the description of the functioning of the lungs. Within the body, vapours rise and accumulate as clouds in the lungs, (the highest point of the lung channel in the chest, is called *yun men*, 雲門, cloud gate), condensing and filtering back through the tissues and passageways to accumulate in the kidneys. This is called the descending of the clear (*qing su* 清肅). The continual action of condensation and diffusion is the most important function of the lung *qi* within the body.

Whereas the sour taste gathers, and has a balancing effect on the expansive nature of the wood *qi*, the pungent taste disperses and diffuses – balancing this contractive effect of the metal. In their double action, the lungs press down, but also diffuse the *qi* to the surface of the skin and the body hair. The lung *qi* is therefore responsible for the quality of the skin, its ability to act as a barrier but also as an intermediary between what is outside and what is within the body. The lung *qi* controls the opening and closing of the pores of the skin.

This relationship between lung *qi* and the skin is an important factor in pathology, where many skin complaints may be associated with the inability of the *qi* of the lungs to correctly diffuse *qi* to the surface of the body. A common clinical example of this close relationship would be a case of childhood asthma and eczema.

The dryness associated with the autumn and the metal element may also be seen in the skin and other peripheral aspects such as hair and nails. In this case, there is not enough moisture reaching the surface areas of the body, which may be due to a deficiency of the lung *qi*. The surface of the skin is affected because of this lack of diffusion. The text continues:

'Of colours it is white
Of sounds it is sobbing
Of reactions to change it is coughing
Of orifices it is the nose…
Of expressions of will, it is oppressive grief.'

The white colour suggests purity and clarity and the bright shine of metal – but it is also related to death. The gate of the year that lies between autumn and winter is the gate of ghosts (*gui men* 鬼 門). The autumn is traditionally associated with sadness, the natural movement of *qi* in autumn being to press down and contract. The text of Suwen 5 accentuates this association with loss, with grief, sadness and sobbing.

Oppressive grief (*you* 憂) suggests a restriction, a constriction, a pressure over the heart which constricts the *qi* in the chest. The breathing becomes shallow and the lungs constrained. There is a cutting off, a loss of engagement with life. Both coughing and sobbing are a kind of reaction to this pressure and restriction of the lungs and the breath.

The regulator of rhythms
In the hierarchy of the organs the lungs are the minister and chancellor, but they are also called the judge and the regulator. Suwen chapter 8:

'The lungs are minister and chancellor
The regulation of all rhythms (*jie* 節) stem from them'[70]

The lungs are the great regulators of the *qi*. The breath is linked to those unconscious body functions – the beating of the heart, the movements along the digestive tract, the opening and closing of the pores. All these rhythms and regulations are under the authority of the lungs.

The character *jie* (節), used here for rhythms, is also used to describe the rhythms of the year, the 24 periods (or *jie*) of the calendar. It is also found in descriptions of the progressions and stages of the circulatory network of the *mai* (脈), the movement of *qi* through the meridians. It is a term used to describe the natural and rhythmical way in which things progress. The character contains the radical for bamboo, and the meaning of *jie* is often associated with the regularity and pattern of the growth of the bamboo plant. What are often called the knots or nodes of *qi* along the pathways of the meridians at each stage (or *jie*) are reflected in the way the bamboo grows straight and then knots together forming a kind of joint before continuing its growth. This pattern of growth and consolidation is often used as an image of the natural flow of life in its *yin* and *yang* phases. We see in Suwen chapter 9:

'The lung is the trunk in which the *qi* is rooted.'[71]

This same text cites the heart as the root of life, the spleen as the root of nutrition, the liver as the root of muscular strength and the kidneys as the root of storage. This association of the lung with the *qi* is its primal

---

70 The Secret Treatise of the Spiritual Orchid, p. 49

71 The Lung, p. 46

function. In some contexts the breath is the *qi*; the lung and the spleen (its *tai yin* 太 陰 partner) working together to provide the basis of post-heaven *qi*. The pooling of *qi* in the chest gives rise to the pulsations and circulations which spread the *qi* and blood throughout the network of the *mai* – beginning with the lung meridian. We take the pulses on the lung meridian, at *qi kou* (氣 口) the mouth of the *qi*, where the *qi* gathers in the great chasm (*tai yuan* 太 淵) of Lung 9. The 'regulation of rhythms' in the text of Suwen 8 are the rhythms of the *qi*. The lungs are often referred to as a bellows, and as such, they stoke the fire of *ming men*, the *yang* of the kidneys, with the breath.

> 'The lung is the source of the *qi* of life; the flowering canopy for the five *zang*… it is the bellows of the forge of the body.'[72]

In the following line of Suwen 9 we read:

> 'It is the residence of the *po*.'

The *po* (魄) are one of the five subtle aspects associated with the five *zang*, they also form a close *yin yang* association with the *hun* (魂). Looking at the character, we may recognize the left part as that of the *gui* (鬼), or ghosts, which tend to come a bit too close for comfort at the end of the autumn. The radical – on the left – is the character *bai* (白) – white. They share the radical *gui* with the *hun*, and in this dual relationship, the *hun* are seen as the spirits related to heaven and the *shen*, while the *po* are those related more closely with the earth and the *jing*, essences. Within the medical texts, these 'white ghosts' are an aspect of the intangible

---

72 Hua Tuo, quoted in The Lung, p. 84

associated with the lungs and with the metal element, and are related to the intelligence innate within the body which governs the automatic body processes – an idea which is close to the Western concept of the autonomic nervous system. As with the other spiritual aspects, we will look at the *po* more closely in a later section, but it is important here to make the association with the breath, and the basic rhythms of life. The lungs, and here the *po*, control the rhythm of the breathing, the impulse to take an in-breath once the out-breath is released. This intake and release of the breath in inhalation and exhalation sets the rhythm for all openings and closings through the body, particularly the gates and doors of the digestive tract, which move food through its various stages of ingestion, assimilation and finally evacuation through the *po men* (魄門) or door of the *po*, one of the names given to the anus.

The lungs master the *qi*, they are responsible for the rhythms and regulations of *qi* and blood, they diffuse vapours, both downwards to the kidneys and outwards to the surface of the skin. As such they are responsible for both the very inner aspects of being and the most superficial. They control the opening and closing of the pores, ensuring defence at the exterior, and are therefore related to the *wei qi*; with the spleen they provide the basis for post-natal *qi*, and therefore contribute to the *ying qi*; the welling-up of *qi* at the sea of *qi* in the chest is responsible for the rhythms of the heart and lungs – and they are therefore intimately connected with the *zong qi*. They command the *qi* at all levels of the body, instigating its cyclical flow through the meridians. Their flowery canopy protects the other *zang*, shading them like a sunshade, while at the same time collecting the vapours which irrigate all the tissues and allow the free exchange of nutrients throughout the system.

Fig. 9 Five element correspondences in Neijing Suwen chapter 5

	WOOD	FIRE	EARTH	METAL	WATER
DIRECTION	east	south	centre	west	north
CLIMATE	wind	heat	damp	dry	cold
TASTE	sour	bitter	sweet	pungent	salty
ZANG	liver	heart	spleen	lung	kidneys
BODY PART	muscular movement	circulation	flesh	skin/body hair	bone
ORIFICE	eyes	tongue	mouth	nose	ears
SOUND	shouting	laughing	singing	sobbing	sighing
REACTION	contraction	oppression	belching	coughing	shivering
WILL	anger	elation	thought	oppression	fear

THE SIX FU:
YANG ORGANS OF TRANSMISSION AND TRANSFORMATION

Neijing Lingshu chapter 52:

> 'The five *zang* (臟) store (*cang* 藏) essences and spirits (*jing shen* 精神), *hun* and *po* (魂 魄). The six *fu* (腑) receive liquid and grain, promote circulation (*xing* 行) and transform (*hua* 化) substances.'[73]

The character *fu* (府) – which is found in the classical texts both with or without the flesh radical – is generally translated as a storehouse or depository. But whereas the *zang* store or treasure in order to keep and guard within (*cang* 藏), the *fu* act more like a depot, where substances may be kept for a while, worked on in some way, but are always in motion, just passing through.

The *fu* are usually listed as a group of six and include the stomach, the gallbladder, the small intestine, the large intestine, the bladder and the function known in Chinese as *san jiao* (三 焦), variously translated as triple heater, triple warmer, triple burner. Because of its wide ranging, and sometimes disputed, function, the triple heater will have its own section at the end of this chapter. Suwen 11 lists just five *fu*, but here it is the gallbladder which is omitted. It is presented earlier in the chapter as one of the 'extraordinary *fu*' – a distinct group of bodily functions/physical structures which will also be discussed under a separate heading.

---

73 From lecture notes: The Fu; Claude Larre and Elisabeth Rochat de la Vallée

Neijing Suwen chapter 11:

> 'The stomach, large intestine, small intestine, triple heater and bladder – these five are produced by the *qi* of heaven. Their *qi* reflect the image of heaven (*tian* 天, nature, the natural order) which is why they make things flow but do not store. Their name is the *fu* of transmission and transformation (*chuan hua zhi fu* 傳 化 之 府).'[74]

This is a very clear description of the difference between the activity of the *zang* and *fu*: the *zang* with the function of storing, which reflects the activity of the *yin qi*, and of the earth; the *fu* that of movement and transformation, which reflects the activity of the *yang qi* and of heaven. Chapter 11 goes on to describe how the *zang* are always full, but the *fu* are full and then empty in succession.

Similarly in Suwen chapter 47:

> 'The five *zang* store the essences and spirits, blood and *qi*, *hun* and *po*; the six *fu* transform the fluids and grains and circulate the interstitial fluids (*jin ye* 津 液).'[75]

The *fu*, whether we count five or six, are essentially concerned with the processing of food and the evacuation of waste. It is of utmost importance in this process that there is constant movement and transformation, with no stagnation; the 'gates and doors' of the digestive tract must be appropriately opened and closed as liquids and grains are transmitted

---

74 ibid.

75 ibid.

from one organ to another. But it is equally important that there is not too rapid a transit, as that may not allow for adequate breakdown and absorption.

The other term associated with the *fu* is *qi hua* (氣 化). From the breakdown of food, nutrients are obtained which move into the bloodstream. There is also a filtration of fluids. But throughout this process – and in various ways – *qi* is produced. Each one of the organs of digestion and assimilation plays a part in the extraction of energy from food, and it is the function of the triple heater to ensure the continuity and regulation of this process.

THE STOMACH *wei* 胃

The stomach is so closely associated with the spleen and the earth element, that we have already seen much of its function in our study of the spleen. This is the only *zang/fu* couple to be paired together in chapter 8 of the Suwen:

> 'The spleen and stomach have the charge of storehouses and granaries. The five tastes stem from them.'[76]

The spleen and stomach work closely together in the process of receiving, breaking down and distributing the nourishment from food. The action of the stomach is sometimes called 'the rotting and ripening

---

76 The Secret Treatise of the Spiritual Orchid, p. 109

of food', an expression which describes well the churning action of the stomach and the breakdown of food stuffs by gastric juices to prepare them for digestion. The stomach manages the more material side of this process, the spleen the more energetic. The spleen acts on the *qi* received from food, raising the most pure elements to the upper heater, where it combines with the *qi* of respiration. The stomach, meanwhile, gets on with the more mundane job of preparing the material elements of food that will be passed on through the digestive tract. The work of the spleen is to 'ascend the clear', that of the stomach to 'descend the unclear', or more dense aspects of food.

The stomach is referred to as 'the sea of nourishment' or the 'sea of liquids and grains'; it is also called 'the sea of the five *zang* and six *fu*', as we see in the following Lingshu chapters:

Lingshu chapter 33:

'The stomach is the sea of liquids and grains. Its influential points are above at *qi jie* (氣 街 Stomach 30) and below at *san li* (三 里 Stomach 36).'[77]

Lingshu chapter 30:

'The six *qi* of the human body are essences (*jing* 精), *qi* (氣), body fluids (*jin ye* 津 液), blood (*xue* 血) and vital circulation (*mai* 脈). The stomach is the great sea for all of this.'[78]

---

77 Spleen and Stomach, p. 121
78 ibid. p. 120

And also in Lingshu chapter 60:

> 'The stomach is the sea of *qi* and blood which come from liquids and grains.'[79]

The image of the sea suggests a great pooling of resources, but also of the constant evaporation of fluids as the sea is warmed. The image of continual vaporization and condensation describe the production of *qi* and the relationship between *qi* and fluids so essential within the Chinese understanding of physiology. Lingshu chapter 56 describes the stomach acting as a sea, with the *ying* (營 nutritive/constructive) and *wei* (衛 defensive) *qi* being produced from that:

> 'The stomach is the sea of the five *zang* and six *fu*; liquids and grains all enter the stomach. The five *zang* and six *fu* all receive the *qi* of the stomach – the five tastes each going to their own place. The *qi* of grains with a sour taste go by preference to the liver. Those of the bitter taste go to the heart, those of sweet grains to the spleen, those of acrid to the lung, and those of salty to the kidneys. The *qi* of the grains and the body fluids (*jin ye* 津 液) that come from them, circulate. The nutritive and defensive *qi* (*ying wei* 營 衛) circulates freely everywhere. Through the process of transformation, there are residues and wastes which are directed below as they should be.'[80]

The stomach is therefore in control of both the nourishment of the five *zang* by the most subtle essences of food (*jing wei* 精 微) via the

---

79 ibid. p. 122

80 ibid. p. 142

spleen, and the production of body fluids and the transformation of the less refined aspects of food into *wei qi*. Once all nutrients have been extracted, the waste is evacuated.

As the close partner of the spleen, jointly governing the centre, and resonating with the element of the earth, the stomach is the basis of post-heaven *qi*. With the spleen it governs the flesh, giving the body its shape and tone. It nourishes the muscles (many pathologies of muscle weakness are related to the stomach and a lack of nourishment), and brings stability to the four limbs; it nourishes the skin, bringing radiance into the face.

The stomach channel is the *yang ming* (陽 明 bright *yang*), and it is related to the large intestine, with which it completes a hand/foot circuit. The stomach channel runs on the front of the body – usually the domain of the *yin* – possibly reflecting its crucial role in nutrition, though still maintaining a *yang* function in relation to its earth partner the spleen. The term *yang ming* is widely used for the function of the stomach and its close relationship to the large intestine in the processing of food and elimination of waste.

THE GALLBLADDER *dan* 膽

The gallbladder has a special place amongst the *fu*; it is not part of the alimentary canal as such – though it aids the breakdown of food and assimilation of essences. It is called the *fu* of the pure and clear. It stores a precious substance, which enables the efficient functioning of the *fu*. In Suwen chapter 11, it is listed amongst the 'extraordinary and permanent *fu*' (*qi heng zhi fu* 奇 恆 之 府) because it stores essences. We will look briefly at the gallbladder here, but it will also be mentioned later in this context.

In its role as an ordinary *fu*, it is paired with the liver and governs the *yang* aspect of the wood element. Unlike the spleen and stomach, the gallbladder and the liver are treated separately in Suwen chapter 8, where the gallbladder is given an interesting charge:

> 'The gallbladder is responsible for what is just and exact (*zhong zheng* 中正); determination (*jue* 決) and decision (*duan* 斷) stem from it.'[81]

The gallbladder acts with precision and exactitude. It is capable of minute adjustment and presides over a kind of inner alignment. It follows the liver very closely, but brings accuracy and definition – control – to the wood energy. In the same chapter, the liver is said to 'assess circumstances and makes plans'. The gallbladder brings the details to those plans and decides how they should be carried out. Determination (*jue* 決) and decision (*duan* 斷) suggest an ability to overcome obstacles and move forward in a correct and precise way.

As the *yang* aspect of the wood energy, the gallbladder often comes first in describing the movement through the five phases – it is the young *yang*, and represents beginnings. It assures that life begins on the right track, adhering to the instructions from the origin. Working with its *shao yang* partner the triple heater, it remains close to 'ministerial fire' and the fire of *ming men*. It is the first stem (*jia* 甲) within the cycles of the stems and branches, which make up the Chinese calendar.

Young *yang* is full of the impetus apparent at the beginning of spring, it has a great strength and determination, pushing through obstacles to

---

81 The Secret Treatise of the Spiritual Orchid, p. 73

come to birth. But it is also seen in the small adjustments which might be made, either within the body or the psyche, to keep things on track – even a small adjustment may move the life in quite a different direction. This is reflected in the movement of the gallbladder meridian which zigzags over the sides of the body and the head, where it has many connections to the brain.

Within common language, to have a strong gallbladder is to have resolve, to be determined, and to be firmly grounded. The character for the gallbladder (*dan* 膽) also means to be courageous. We often find within the Chinese description of body/mind that it is the gallbladder's rooting in the origin that allows for movement and change. If the gallbladder is weak, there will be a lack of resolve, and a tendency towards all kinds of small deviations from the norm. The body may be unable to come back to its correct state after an illness. Maybe it no longer knows what its correct state is. There may be unfounded fears and apprehensions.

In its role as an ordinary *fu*, the ability of the gallbladder to be just and exact is reflected in its action on the digestive juices and enzymes, so vital in the breakdown and absorption of food. Because it stores 'essential juices' (*jing zhi* 精 汁) it has a connection to the origins of life, and carries the patterning of, or information from, the origin. It is therefore part of the intelligence required in this sorting and refining process – the process that ensures that what is taken in can be correctly processed in order to become an integral part of us.

Resonating with the wood element and therefore with wind, disturbance of the gallbladder may manifest in symptoms which come and go, move around – there may be alternation of heat and cold. The gallbladder is often called the pivot between what is inside and what is outside. It is a *fu* that acts as a *zang* in its ability to store, and may therefore be seen as an intermediary between the *zang* and *fu*. As the *shao yang* meridian, it is seen to pivot between back and front, inner and outer, making connections to both the *yin* and *yang* channels. The influential points (*mu* points) of the kidneys are found on the gallbladder meridian, and yet it also brings clear *yang* to the brain. The gallbladder thus balances the *biao li* (表 裡) – the movement towards the exterior and the movement towards the interior. This will be discussed further when we look at its role as an 'extraordinary *fu*'.

THE SMALL INTESTINE *xiao chang* 小腸

The function of the small intestine is linked with the fire element and the heart. Its meridian is the *tai yang* (greater *yang* 太陽), forming a circuit with the bladder. The presentation in Suwen chapter 8 puts the small intestine after the large – but this was not because of a misunderstanding of physiology. In the classical Chinese, what is large or great necessarily comes before what is small! The Chinese certainly understood that the small intestine absorbed nutrients while the large intestine was more concerned with waste, but they also understood the role of the large intestine in reclaiming fluids. In Lingshu chapter 10 it is suggested that the small intestine meridian (hand *tai yang*) is in charge of the *ye* (液) fluids, the rich dense fluids full of essences, which circulate in the depths of the body, while the large intestine meridian (hand *yang ming*) is in charge of the *jin* (津) fluids, which circulate more superficially.[82]

The small intestine has two doors – *you men* (幽門, the dark gate)

---

82 Lecture notes: The Fu

which leads from the stomach (which probably includes the function of the duodenum) into the small intestine, and *lan men* (闌門, the barrier gate) which corresponds to the area of the ileo-caecal valve and is located between the small and large intestine.

> Suwen chapter 8: 'The small intestine is responsible for receiving (*shou* 受) and making things thrive (*sheng* 盛). Transformed substances (*hua wu* 化物) stem from it.'[83]

The small intestine receives from the stomach after the action of the gallbladder. It also 'makes things thrive'. This character *sheng* (盛) is the same that we saw in Suwen chapter 1 in the description of the rising power of the kidneys allowing growth and development throughout the seven and eight year cycles. Here it refers to the ability of the small intestine to extract nutrients from food, to reabsorb them into the body and to ensure the constant renewal and rebuilding of tissues. It does this by transforming substances – a process of filtering, discarding and absorbing which allows continual growth, change and transformation within the body structure.

The link between the small intestine, the fire element and the heart suggests some kind of discriminating intelligence. In the Nanjing it is called the 'red intestine', and it is closely associated with the quality of the blood. The intelligence that is shown by the fire of the heart in mental clarity, an ability to discriminate between sensory impressions via the upper orifices, and in emotional balance – is seen in the small intestine on a more physical level. It is the ability to sort the clear from the unclear (*bie qing zhuo* 別清濁); to know what to absorb and what to reject in

---

83 *The Secret Treatise of the Spiritual Orchid*, p. 119

order to replenish the nutrients within the blood. It is a body intelligence that allows for discrimination.

In Lingshu chapter 47, the small intestine is linked with the heart and the *mai* (脈, vital circulation):

'The heart makes a junction (*he* 合) with the small intestine; the response of the small intestine is in the *mai* (脈).'[84]

The link between the heart and small intestine, and between the small intestine and its meridian are difficult to comprehend in terms of Western physiology, though recent research has suggested possible connections via the lymph system.[85] In the classical texts, very little is said concerning their relationship. While the functions of the *zang* are well explained within the five-fold system of the elements/phases, those of the *fu* are more speculative. Certainly within Suwen chapter 5, which defines *wu xing* correspondences, there is no mention of the *fu*. And while the functions of spleen and stomach are closely linked within the earth element, liver and gallbladder to the wood and kidneys and bladder to water – the two intestines are rarely mentioned in terms of their five phase relationships, or to their element partners. The historical shifts in pulse positions for the two intestines also suggests a lack of stability in their positioning amongst the *zang fu*.

We might also wonder about the connection between these two meridians located on the arms, neck and face, and the organs located in the lower belly. The most commonly mentioned points in the classical literature for treatment of the small and large intestines respectively are

---

84 Lecture notes: The Fu

85 The Pairing of Heart and Small Intestine, *Xin xiao chang xiang biao*; on-line article by Dr. Electra Peluffo (www.electrapeluffo.com)

on the stomach channel: Stomach 37 (*ju xu shang lian* 巨 虛 上 廉) and 39 (*ju xu xia lian* 巨 虛 下 廉).

The front *mu* point of the small intestine, Ren 4, is traditionally associated with the nourishment of the blood, which complements the function of the small intestine to absorb nutrients from food into the blood. But this point is called *guan yuan* (關 原) the gate or pass to the origin, and it has connections to the kidneys and to the uterus. A research project conducted in Japan in the 1980s, tested over 800 women in the early stages of pregnancy with a computerized 'akabane' type process of assessing comparative meridian strength.[86] It was the small intestine meridian which consistently showed a significant increase in *qi*, suggesting a close connection with the uterus. There is much to think on here – and this subject will continue to be a rich area for both research and speculation.

THE LARGE INTESTINE *da chang* 大 腸

The large intestine runs from *lan men* (闌 門), the barrier gate in the area of the ileo-caecal valve, to *po men* (粕 門) the gate of waste, or the anus. It is sometimes described as the 'turning intestine' (*hui chang* 迴 腸).

In Suwen chapter 8 it is said:

'The large intestine is responsible for transit (*chuan dao* 傳 道).

---

86 Institute for Human Science, Tokyo

Change and transformation (*bian hua* 變化) stem from it.'[87]

A later commentary enlarges on this:

'The large intestine commands transmission and transformation (*chuan hua* 傳化) of residues and waste (*zao po* 糟粕); its role is to ensure transit (*chuan dao* 傳道) and to change and transform (*bian hua* 變化).'[88]

The large intestine continues the work of the small intestine, but rather than assimilating essences, it is more concerned with fluids – deciding what to reabsorb and what to excrete. It is important for the large intestine to have the correct balance of fluid – too dry and there may be constipation, too much fluid and there may be loose stools, and not enough fluid is retained. The large intestine is said (by later commentators) to be connected to the *jin* fluids, which circulate in the more superficial pathways, in the skin and interstitial spaces. The skin may be dry if the large intestine is not carrying out this function of reclaiming fluids correctly. This is a further function of the separation of the clear and unclear which takes place within the *fu*.

Lingshu chapter 47 reminds us of the connection within the metal element with the skin:

'The lung makes a junction with the large intestine. It is in the skin that the large intestine has its response (*ying* 應).'[89]

---

[87] The Secret Treatise of the Spiritual Orchid, p. 115
[88] The Fu: lecture notes
[89] ibid.

The same chapter that suggests a response between the blood circulatory system and the small intestine, here suggests a response between the skin and the lung and large intestine. This connection is seen in the five phase resonances to the metal element, and many treatments strategies for skin problems use both lung and large intestine meridians. The character *ying* (應) translated above as to respond, is the term commonly used for the five element resonances or correspondences. It is to resonate with, to respond to – a cause in one thing creating an effect in another, for example. Within the *zang fu*, this kind of mutual resonance is the way in which symptoms observable at the surface of the body may suggest a disturbance within an inner organ system, which would otherwise be difficult to detect. This enables the practitioner to diagnose a problem within the *qi* of a specific organ system before any physical manifestation within the organ itself.

The acupuncture point most commonly mentioned within the Neijing and Jiayijing for treatment of the large intestine is its lower *he* (合) or junction point, Stomach 37 (*ju xu shang lian* 巨 虛 上 廉), reinforcing the idea that we see in many texts, that the stomach controls the digestive process, from beginning to end. The front *mu* point of the large intestine is also on the stomach channel (Stomach 25) – which has the slightly surprising name of celestial, or heavenly pivot (*tian shu* 天 樞); surprising because the character heaven tends to appear only in the names of acupuncture points in the upper part of the body. This is the lowest point to contain the character, suggesting its great importance in the process of transformation and transportation.

The anus, or gate of the *po*, is usually written with the character for waste (*po* 粕) but it can also be seen with the character of the bodily soul, or *yin* soul (*po* 魄). The *po* is the aspect of spirit or intelligence which is most closely related to the physical body. In the medical texts, it is associated with the metal element and the lung and large intestine, and one of its functions is to regulate peristalsis – the rhythmic movement which allows the churning of the food as it is successively broken down, as well as the opening and closing of the gates and doors of the digestive tract, which moves the bolus of food from one *fu* to another. At death, the *po* is said to leave the body via the anus, the gate of the *po*.

As their *yang ming* (陽明 bright *yang*) pairing suggests, the stomach and large intestine work closely together in all aspects of digestion. They are said to be rich in both blood and *qi*. In a way theirs is a more mundane role, that of churning and moving, whereas the small intestine has the more discriminatory role of absorbing the appropriate essences, of sifting and sorting. But the stomach and large intestine make sure that this all works well.

THE BLADDER *pang guang* 膀胱

The bladder is the *fu* paired with the kidneys within the water element. This may seem straightforward after the convolutions of the intestines, but within Chinese medicine, the function of the bladder is also full of strange contradictions. Small, and in many ways insignificant amongst the internal organs, its channel is the longest, and it is designated the great *yang* (太陽 *tai yang*) – its pathway, doubling on the back, contains the back *shu* points, major acupuncture points for treating all the *zang fu*.

The bladder is presented in the final position in Suwen chapter 8, possibly echoing its lowly place in the hierarchy of the organs, but also stressing its ability, through its meridian, to draw them all together into a cohesive whole.

> 'The bladder is responsible for regions and cities (*zhou du* 州 都); it stores the body fluids (*jin ye* 津 液); the transformations of *qi* (*qi hua* 氣 化) then give out their power.'[90]

The character *zhou* (州), translated as regions, suggests a division of water from land. Once that is accomplished, a city (*du* 都) may be established. We have seen previously the importance of irrigation and drainage in China at this time; the ability to secure a city from floods, while remaining close enough to a river to make use of its irrigation and transportation, was a main preoccupation of government agencies. Suwen chapter 8 – modelled on the structure of the imperial court – reflects this within the presentation of the *fu*. Within the body, the process of separating liquid from solid, clear from unclear, finally ends with the bladder, which stores the body fluids and regulates them, by evacuating what is no longer needed and reabsorbing what can be recycled. At the end of this whole process of transformation, the *qi* are able to give out their power. The power of the *qi* is seen in the magnificence of the bladder channel, the great *yang*, which threads together the *zang fu* like pearls on a string as it doubles and redoubles along the back.

The action of the bladder within Chinese medicine is on all the fluids in the lower belly. But the fluids from the small and large intestine are sent to the bladder to be transformed – so its function is not simply one of evacuation. The bladder shares this control of liquids with the triple heater, which, as we see in Lingshu chapter 47, may also be linked to the kidneys:

---

90 The Secret Treatise of the Spiritual Orchid, p. 146

'The kidneys make a junction with the triple heater (*san jiao* 三 焦) and the bladder; their response (*ying* 應) is seen in the *cou li* (腠 理) and the *hao mao* (毫 毛).'[91]

The Nanjing texts suggest that the right kidney is linked with *ming men* and the element fire; its associated *fu* is the triple heater. The left kidney is linked with water and its associated *fu* is the bladder. If the bladder controls the quality and quantity of the liquids, the triple heater controls their movement and transformation. This also reflects the common pulse positioning, where the *yang* aspect of the kidneys, sometimes referred to as *ming men*, is paired with the triple heater on the right wrist, while the *yin* of the kidneys, the kidneys in their water aspect, is paired with the bladder on the left. We will look at this more closely in discussing the triple heater.

Cou li (as it is seen in the text of Lingshu 47 above) is a difficult term to translate, but the character *li* (理) suggests that what is within, and part of an inner patterning, may be seen at the surface in subtle ways, in particular markings and folds – the etymology of the character implies that the markings on the surface of a piece of jade (玉) show its inner structure (里). A skilled craftsperson is able to read these markings and know how best to carve the jade. *Cou* (腠) refers to the layers of the skin. In classical texts, *cou li* suggests the texture of the skin, which gives so much information about the inner state of the body. In modern medical dictionaries, the *cou li* is the space between the skin and the muscle – possibly the connective tissues, or the water rich areas of the dermis, which modern Japanese research speculates to be the area where

---

91 The Fu; text of Lingshu 47 from lecture handout

meridians flow.[92]

Hao mao (毫毛) is more simply translated as the body hair, or down, the very fine hairs which grow from the pores of the skin. Classical texts more usually cite the skin and body hair as linked with the lung, as we saw in Suwen chapter 5, where the more usual term *pi mao* (皮毛) is used. *Cou li* and *hao mao* are more complex terms and suggest the action of the bladder in returning the filtered fluids back into the system, and the ability to carry them to the surface of the skin by way of the various systems of irrigation and diffusion. The lung and the bladder share this function of both moistening and guarding the exterior at the surface of the skin.

The bladder is much more than a depository for waste fluids. Within the Chinese perspective it plays a major role in the filtering and recycling of precious fluids; it works closely with the kidneys and the triple heater, and also the lung, which sends fluids down through a process of filtration, as well as moistening the skin. By its meridian, the *tai yang*, it is the main controller of the diffusion of *yang qi*, acting closely with the governor vessel (*du mai* 督脈). Running either side of the spine, with close links to the kidneys, the bladder meridian plays an important role in the regulation and irrigation of the nervous system and the brain.

As we move on to look at the triple heater, we will see that as the stomach, small intestine and large intestine act together in their role of digestion and absorption, so the gallbladder, triple heater and bladder all have a role in the transformation of *qi*.

---

92 Institute for Human Science, Tokyo

TRIPLE HEATER: SAN JIAO

The triple heater (*san jiao* 三焦) has no equivalent in Western anatomy or physiology, and has been described in different ways within a variety of texts and commentaries throughout the history of the medical literature. So even within the context of Chinese medicine, this is not an easy notion to grasp. In the early chapters of the Neijing, *san jiao* is listed as one of the six *fu* – the organs of digestion and transmission, circulation and transformation, and it is often referred to in relation to the circulation of fluids. Suwen chapter 8 says very simply:

'The triple heater is responsible for circulation and irrigation. The waterways stem from it.'[93]

But in the texts of the Nanjing, we see the triple heater as closely related to original *qi*, and to the fire of *ming men* – and as something with 'name but no form'. This conglomeration of information, once seen in context, provides a fascinating impression of this elusive function. In all its representations, it encompasses the whole, and could possibly be an early attempt to explain something of the way in which the body works

---

93 The Secret Treatise of the Spiritual Orchid, p. 142

as a unity through its various parts. According to Ming dynasty physician Zhang Jiebin:

> 'The triple heater, though it is the *fu* of all drainage and irrigation of the middle, it is also that which gathers together and protects all the *yang*… there is nothing that it does not envelop and surround.'[94]

This role of gathering together and protecting the *yang* and the important relationship with the fire element, is reflected in the character translated as warmer, heater or burner – *jiao* (焦). The four strokes at the bottom represent the fire radical, which takes different forms depending on its position within the character. Here, at the bottom, it suggests a slow warming heat – like a fire under a cooking pot. The upper part of the character originally has the meaning of a type of bird, and it is suggested that it represents the layering of feathers to create an interlocking protective covering.[95] With the thread radical on the left (維), the character has the meaning of layers and networks of connections, reflecting Zhang Jiebin's statement, '…there is nothing that it does not envelop and surround'.

Within the chapters of the Neijing, the triple heater is described in relation to the ways that *qi* and fluids act and move within three distinct areas of the body: the upper heater, the area above the diaphragm, which includes the heart and the lungs; the middle heater, which deals with digestion and includes the stomach and spleen, liver and gallbladder; the lower heater, which includes the kidneys, bladder and intestines. The upper heater is described as an area of vapours; the middle heater as a place for the breaking down of food; the lower heater as a collection of

---

94 Heart Master Triple Heater, p. 58
95 Wieger's Chinese Characters, Lesson 168 A

channels and ditches for irrigation and drainage:

> 'The upper heater is like a mist (*wu* 霧), the middle heater is like a maceration (*ou* 漚), the lower heater is like a drainage ditch (*du* 瀆).'[96]

The upper heater

The heart and lungs share the space above the diaphragm with the more elusive *tan zhong*, the central palace or sea of *qi* in the chest. This is the area of the most refined *qi*, the diaphragm acting as a kind of filter, which allows only the purest *qi* and essences into the rarified atmosphere of the emperor and his minister.

Here the *qi* is like a mist, and the canopy of the lungs at the top of the chest spreads out to diffuse the vapours and allow a percolation down through the waterways, irrigating the tissues and flesh. *Tan zhong* is the palace of the *zong qi*, the ancestral or gathering *qi*, which gives the pulsating rhythms to the heart, the breath and the circulation of *qi* throughout the meridians. The meridian of the triple heater has a direct connection with *tan zhong*, where it also connects to its *yin* partner, *xin zhu* (pericardium). The upper heater is a drawing together of all that we have seen of the heart and the lungs, *tan zhong* and *zong qi*.

The middle heater

The middle heater is called a maceration, which is a good description of the process of 'rotting and ripening' of food – the churning around and breaking down, in order to release all nutrients. This is the realm of

---

96 Lingshu chapter 18 in Heart Master Triple Heater, p. 73

the spleen and stomach, and it is here that the activity of *qi* production begins. Post-natal *qi* refers to the continual renewal of energy through the processes of assimilation and reconstruction which begin within the middle heater. It is here that we find the second of the four seas – the sea of liquids and grains, and also come across the term *jing wei* (精微), the most subtle essences of food, which are closely related to the nutritive/constructive or *ying qi*. It is within the middle heater, that these most subtle essences of food are raised by the spleen to the upper heater, and the more dense are moved downwards by the stomach for further breakdown, assimilation or evacuation in the lower heater. These most subtle of essences are also associated with the production of blood, which has its foundation in the middle heater.

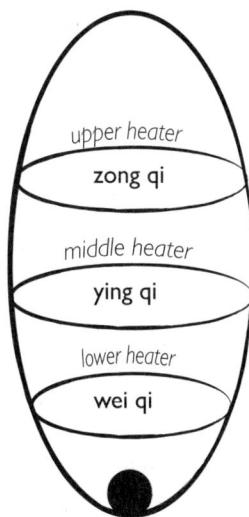

Fig 10: *The three jiao – wei qi, ying qi, zong qi*

The lower heater

The lower warming space is described quite simply as a drainage ditch, but within this ditch, water is redistributed, filtered, osmosed, warmed and cooled, vaporized and condensed. It is stored within the tissues or released as vapours which irrigate the surface of the body. The defensive or *wei qi* is made here, from the less subtle essences of food, transformed by the action of the fire of *ming men*. So fluids are filtered, the most unclear being passed on for evacuation, and all that can be reclaimed, recycled throughout the system.

Fire and water

The descriptions in the Neijing, and particularly in Suwen chapter 8, provide an understanding of the triple heater as responsible for fluids and for the circulation of fluids within the system, but the triple heater is much more than a simple irrigation system. It is in the careful balance of fire and water that it is able to control fluids, but also to release mists and vapours, as in a slow, gentle cooking process.

The triple heater is associated with the fire element, and has a *yin yang, biao/li* relationship with the *xin zhu* (the second aspect of the heart, literally heart as master, which is generally referred to as the pericardium), as we can see in Nanjing difficulty 25:

> 'The *xin zhu* (心 主) and the *san jiao* (三 焦) are related internally/externally (*biao/li* 表 理).'[97]

The triple heater has a close relationship with *ming men huo*, the fire of

---

97 Heart Master Triple Heater, p. 34

the gate of life. This is fire in its 'ministerial' role, not the sovereign fire of the heart/mind, calm container for the spirits, but fire in its warming, invigorating, activating mode. In this role, the triple heater radiates the transformational fire of *ming men* throughout the whole body, warming the flesh, diffusing fluids, maintaining metabolism. It has a particular resonance with the areas of protection and connection around the heart, (*xin bao luo* 心 包 絡) and with the heart in its active role of circulating blood and *qi* (*xin zhu mai* 心 主 脈).

The triple heater and yuan qi

In the Nanjing, the triple heater is related to original *qi* and to the '*qi* that moves between the kidneys', which is possibly another way to describe *ming men*. This is seen in the text of Nanjing difficulty 8:

> 'The twelve meridians (*jing mai* 經 脈) are connected with the source (*yuan* 原) of the generative *qi* (*sheng qi* 生 氣). The source of the generative *qi* is the root and foundation of the twelve meridians, that is the *qi* that moves between the kidneys (*shen jian dong qi* 腎 間 動 氣). This *qi* is the foundation of the five *zang* and the six *fu*, the root of the twelve meridians, the gate of exhalation and inhalation, the source (*yuan* 原) of the triple heater. It is also called the spirit that guards against perverse influences (*shou xie zhi shen* 守 邪 之 神).'[98]

This connection is further elaborated in Nanjing difficulty 66, where the triple heater is described as the agent for the distribution of original *qi*:

---

98 ibid. p. 106

'The *qi* that moves between the kidneys, below the navel, is the life and destiny (*sheng ming* 生 命) of a human being. It is the root and foundation of the twelve meridians. Hence it is called original (*yuan* 原). The three heaters are the agents for the distribution of original *qi* (*yuan qi* 原 氣). They govern the free circulation of the three *qi* and their passage through the five *zang* and the six *fu*.'[99]

So the triple heater is presented in these texts as a kind of messenger from the vital source of life, close to the beginnings of things and the root of the breath. It circulates original *qi* throughout the three distinct areas of the body under its control, and in doing so controls and circulates the three *qi*, *zong qi*, *ying qi* and *wei qi*.

Form and no-form

This expansive understanding of the triple heater is further expressed in the text of Nanjing difficulty 25, which connects *san jiao* and *xin zhu* in their minister fire *yin yang* relationship, and then goes on to say:

'These two have a name but no form (*wu xing* 無 形)'.[100]

And in later commentaries on this text:

'Form is derived from no-form and then it can function. Therefore the function of the *yin* and *yang* organs and meridians is truly brought about by the function of the master heart (*xin zhu* 心 主) and the

---

99 ibid. p. 113
100 ibid. p. 34

triple heater (*san jiao* 三 焦).'

We have briefly looked at this idea of no-form in the context of the double aspect of the heart. It is not easy to understand, and has been taken to mean different things by commentators over the centuries. In the language of the Nanjing, with its association of the triple heater with *ming men* and original *qi*, we may understand 'no-form' to reflect its meaning within the early philosophical texts, which suggest a state before manifestation, of 'image without form'; the original *qi* or information patterning before matter takes shape. This suggests that the triple heater affects the way in which inherited information is carried into physical form, and that the role of minister fire is to act as a kind of go-between – between pre-heaven and post-heaven, form and no-form.

But there is also an idea, put forward by later commentators, that the idea of no-form literally means that both the *xin zhu/xin bao luo* (as the expression of minister fire connected to the heart), and *san jiao* are not organs as the other *zang fu*, but are formless, shapeless tissues, which both protect and bind around all the other organ systems, providing both connection (*luo* 絡) and protection (*bao* 包).

It is important here to consider the terms *gao* (膏) and *huang* (肓), described variously as a kind of primitive tissue or a greasy paste. In classical descriptions of embryological development, for example in Huainanzi chapter 7, we see that at the first month, the foetus is called *gao* (膏), which Elisabeth Rochat translates as a rich paste, full of essences and the potential for making life.[101] The terms *gao* and *huang* are generally regarded as primitive tissues which are found around the area of the heart and diaphragm and in the area of *ming men* and the navel. The terms are also

---

101 Pregnancy and Gestation, Monkey Press 2007, p. 23

found in a series of point names in these areas, all of which have close links to the *xin zhu* (pericardium) or *san jiao* (triple heater).[102]

Possible embryonic connections between the location of the gate of life, the triple heater and the protective tissues around the heart have been speculated, suggesting a migration of tissues which has been observed within early embryonic development.[103] This primitive tissue seems to be part of the connection and protection system – having a specific relationship to the heart and to *ming men*, the gate of life, but also acting as a kind of protective and connective system for all the internal organs. In the adult, the three heaters are seen as a kind of 'felting' around all the organs – in the same way that there are 'protections' around the heart.

This idea is explored by modern scholars and practitioners who suggest a connection between the triple heater, the *gao huang* and the fascia. This links in well with the concept of communication transfer through the fascia, described, for example, by biologist James Oschman as:

'…biochemically and bio-electrically active chains of tissues, capable of a variety of communication transfers.'[104]

This is a complex subject, in need of more study – but as embryology is able to observe the early stages of foetal development with increasingly more precision, exciting progress will be made in the understanding of these processes – hopefully clarifying some of the interesting but obscure areas

---

102 Bl 43, Gaohuangshu, is on the outer bladder line on the back, in line with the *shu* point of the pericardium. (Bl 15); Huangmen, Bl 51, is in line with the *shu* point of the triple heater. Huangshu, Ki 16, is at the side of the umbilicus.

103 The Survey of Traditional Chinese Medicine, Ricci Institute 1986, p. 209

104 James Oschman, unpublished manuscript; see also James Oschman, Energy Medicine, Churchill Livingstone, 2000

of Chinese medicine which seem to resonate with current embryological findings. Maybe these migrating tissues and the communication through them goes some way to explain the various connections made within the classical texts between the heart and the fire of *ming men*, and with the idea that the triple heater acts as a distributor of *qi* throughout the five *zang* and six *fu*. According to the great physician Sun Simiao:

> 'The three heaters, through their interconnections, make a unity. They govern the way of the spirits, which come and go in the five *zang* and six *fu*. They know how to distribute life in the form of *qi*. They are connected to the origin (*yuan*, source 原) they make blood and maintain life through the spirits.'[105]

---

105 Heart Master Triple Heater, p. 118

THE EXTRAORDINARY AND PERMANENT FU

Suwen chapter 11:

'Brain, marrow, bones, vital circulation, gallbladder and uterus, these six are produced by the *qi* of the earth. They store *yin* and reflect the image of the earth. Their name is *qi heng zhi fu* (奇 恆 之 腑), the extraordinary and permanent *fu*.'[106]

This grouping of functions is mentioned only once in the Neijing, in the above passage from Suwen chapter 11. The character *qi* (奇), translated as extraordinary, suggests something that is apart from the usual classification of things. These are not the ordinary *fu*. Here, as with the eight extraordinary meridians (*qi jing ba mai* 奇 經 八 脈) is

---

106 The Extraordinary Fu, Monkey Press 2003, p. 19

a grouping which is outside of the five element patterning or *yin yang* pairing used to define the functions of the internal organs. *Qi* (奇) means to be special, set apart. The character *heng* (恆) suggests a permanence, something that is reliable and always there. These body functions are also out of the ordinary because they are *fu*, but they act more like *zang*. Some are hollow, but store a precious substance, like the gallbladder, some are not really like *fu* at all – like the marrow and the bones. But they are reliable, always working, maintaining the organism at a deep level.

The brain, the bones, the marrow and the uterus, all have a connection with the kidneys; the gallbladder stores precious essences and the vital circulation (*mai* 脈) contains and circulates the blood. In commentaries on this group of functions, we hear that certain daoist practices of 'embryonic respiration' involved the six extraordinary *fu*[107] – so they may be presumed to have a direct link with the origin. And it is because of this link with the origin, that they assure development and continuity.

THE BRAIN *nao* 腦

The character *nao* (腦) has the flesh radical on the left, denoting a part of the body; on the right, a pictogram of a scull with hair at the top. Hair is a symbol of the strength of the essences, and the brain is the receptacle of pure essences.

In Lingshu chapter 33 the brain is listed as one of the 'four seas':

'Human beings have a sea of marrow, a sea of blood, a sea of *qi* and

---

107 ibid. p. 27

a sea of fluids and grains. …The brain is the sea of marrow, its points are above at the canopy (Du 20) and below at *feng fu* (Du 16).'[108]

And later in the chapter:

'If there is an excess in the sea of marrow, one is alert and robust with a lot of strength. One fills abundantly one's allotted years. If there is insufficiency in the sea of marrow, the brain turns around (vertigo), there is buzzing in the ears and the legs are weak with a kind of paralysis (*jing wei* 經痿). One has visual disturbances and can no longer see. One is slow and likes to lie down quietly.'[109]

As the sea of marrow, the brain is very *yin* and must be animated by the pure *yang*. According to Ming dynasty physician Li Shizhen,[110] the brain is the '*yuan shen zhi fu* (元神之府)', the *fu* of the original spirit, which allows perception. The classical texts do not mention any connection between the brain and thinking as such, it is more a matter of perception, which is facilitated by the clarity of the essences (*jing ming* 精明). *Jing ming* (睛明, clear vision) is the name of the acupuncture point at the inner corner of the eye, which has a connection to the brain and also with a secondary pathway of the heart meridian. It is this relationship with the upper orifices, the modes of perception, the brain and the heart which combine to bring about consciousness. As the sea of marrow, the brain also has a relationship with the kidneys.

In Suwen chapter 17 the reference is simply to the head:

---

108 ibid. p. 56-58
109 ibid. p. 61
110 ibid. p. 81

'The five *zang* and six *fu* are the powerful force of the body. The head (*tou* 頭) is the depot (*fu* 府) of the radiant essences (*jing ming* 精 明). When the head is disturbed, the vision fades, the vital spirit (*jing shen* 精 神) is deprived of force.'[111]

The extraordinary *fu* store the most precious substances – the brain stores the original spirit and the radiant essences.

MARROW and BONES *sui gu* 髓 骨

The brain is the sea of marrow, but the *sui* is the marrow (髓) within the bones (*gu* 骨). Unlike the sea, it has a circulation, and is close to the *ye* of the *jin ye* (津 液 body fluids) – the dense fluids which lubricate and nourish in the depths of the body. In the classical texts, the marrow and bones usually appear as a pair – so we will look at these two of the extraordinary *fu* together.

Suwen chapter 5 tells us that the kidneys generate the bones and marrow. And in Suwen chapter 17, the bones are said to be the *fu* (腑), or depot, of the marrow. The bones provide the structure, shape and force of direction. The marrow is within the bones; made from the essences of the kidneys, it nourishes the bones. Bones and marrow are one of the *yin yang* couples related to the kidneys, representing the hard and the soft. The other most commonly mentioned pair is the teeth and the hair, which closely reflect the cycles of growth and development. As the kidneys are related to the source of life and its development according to

---

111 ibid. p. 43

the information patterning of the original *qi*, problems within the bones and marrow are often related to inherited or developmental issues. Pains in the bones are said to come from an insufficient nourishment by the marrow, and hence an insufficiency of kidney essences.

Brain, bones and marrow relate to each other and to the essences of the kidneys, and as such are close to the foundation and development of life.

THE VITAL CIRCULATION *mai* 脈

The fourth in the list of extraordinary *fu* is the *mai* (脈). This is a very general term to refer to all the possible kinds of circulation of blood and *qi* within the body. Its character is made with the flesh radical, which describes a part of the body, and a phonetic of underground streams and currents of water. We will look at the character in more detail when we discuss the meridian network, but *mai* (脈) gives the idea of an intricate network of pathways and their interconnections.

Suwen chapter 17:

'The *mai* are the *fu* of the blood.'[112]

As the brain is the *fu* (府) of the essences and the original spirits (*yuan shen zhi fu* 元 神 之 府), and the bones the *fu* of the marrow, so the *mai* are the *fu*, or depository, of the blood. We have seen that the heart governs the *mai* (*xin zhu mai* 心 主 脈) and in a commentary on Suwen

---

112 ibid. p. 109

chapter 10:

'The heart produces blood and stores the spirits. When we speak of the *mai*, the substance is the blood, and the effects are in the spirits. Hence the junction of the heart is the *mai*.'[113]

And in Lingshu chapter 8:

'The heart guards the *mai*. The *mai* are the dwelling place of the spirits. When the *qi* of the heart is empty, there is sadness. When it is full, one laughs without stopping.'[114]

Mai is both the vessel and the circulation. The *mai* store and circulate the blood and *qi*, as well as circulating the *ying* (營), the nutritive *qi*. In the Chinese, *mai* refers to the whole meridian network as well as its reflection in the pulse.

UTERUS *bao* 胞

In the context of the extraordinary *fu*, *bao* is generally translated as the uterus, but the term *bao zhong* (胞 中) is also used to express the deep inner structures, closely connected to *ming men* (命 門, life gate), where the first four of the eight extraordinary meridians have their origin. In this context, *bao zhong* relates to both men and women. The term *bao*

---

113 ibid. p. 116
114 ibid. p. 116

is also used to refer to the bladder, and in fact describes any enveloping protective sac.

Nanjing difficulty 36 makes a particular connection between *ming men* and the *bao*, where a distinction is made between male and female, and the meaning is certainly the uterus:

> '*Ming men* (命門) is the residence of the spirits/essences (*shen jing* 神精); it is where the original *qi* (*yuan qi* 原氣) are secured. Man stores (*cang* 藏) essences (*jing* 精, sperm); woman secures the uterus (*bao* 胞).'[115]

The character *bao* (包), without the flesh radical, also appears in the *xin bao luo* (心包絡), the protections and connections of the heart, where it has the meaning of a protective network. Wieger's Chinese Characters explains the etymology of *bao* (包) as the embryo protected within the mother's body; it later had the more general meaning of guarding and protecting something precious. The text of Suwen chapter 33 has an interesting reference to the *bao* as the uterus:

> 'If menstruation (*yue shi* 月事, literally, the monthly affair) does not come, it is because the vital circulation of the uterus (*bao mai* 胞脈) is closed (*bi* 閉). The vital circulation natural to the uterus has a relationship of dependency with the heart and a connection (*luo* 絡) with the central protection of life (*bao zhong* 胞中).'[116]

This translation by Elisabeth Rochat differentiates very well the uterus

---

115 The Kidneys, p. 9

116 The Extraordinary Fu, p. 179

itself and the *bao zhong*, which here represents the protection of the origin of life. The uterus has a connection to that, and also a dependency on the heart. The *bao mai* is all the circulation related to the uterus, but of course particularly here, the circulation of the blood. The *bao mai* regulates the menstrual flow, but also brings blood and nutrients (*ying* 營) to the developing embryo. We will see that the extraordinary meridians *ren* and *chong mai*, which are described as beginning in this place of the protection of the origin of life (*bao zhong*), also play a great part in menstruation and the ability both to conceive, to carry a child to term, and also in the birthing process.

GALLBLADDER *dan* 膽

The character for gallbladder, *dan* (膽), also means to be courageous, and this is reflected in the description in Suwen chapter 8, where the gallbladder is said to be determined, just and exact. As the *yang* partner of the liver, it takes on all the attributes of the wood element, but it is designated as one of the extraordinary and permanent *fu* because of its connection with the origin of life and its ability to store essences. Through its *shao yang* partner the triple heater it is linked to the original fire of *ming men*.

Suwen chapter 9 says that all the eleven *zang fu* go to the gallbladder for direction. Within the heavenly stems (the designated symbols of ten year cycles within Chinese astrology) the gallbladder is related to the first stem (*jia* 甲) and also to the first month of pregnancy. As the *yang* representative of the wood element, it is the initiator.

The gallbladder is counted as one of the ordinary *fu*, but it is also extraordinary because it stores the most pure essences. Lingshu chapter 2:

> 'The gallbladder is the *fu* of the central essences (*zhong jing zhi fu* 中 精 之 府).'[117]

Zhong (中) is literally a pictograph of an arrow hitting the centre of the target: it is to be on the mark, in the right place at the right time. As we saw with the term *bao zhong*, *zhong* (中) does not simply mean to be in the middle – it suggests a central, intrinsic function, something close to the origins of life. The character also conveys a meaning very close to the description of the gallbladder as being just and exact. Other terms of expression for the gallbladder are '*zhong qing zhi fu*' (中 清 之 府), the *fu* of central purity, and '*qing jing zhi fu*' (清 精 之 府), the *fu* of the pure essences. The gallbladder stores the pure and clear essences of the centre; it facilitates the action of the other *fu* in their role of processing food, but it only comes into contact with what is pure and clear in order to remain true to the origin; only that which is pure is able to transmit the original information patterning of the origin.

---

117 ibid. p. 143

THE EMOTIONS: QING

Neijing Suwen chapter 5:

'Heaven has four seasons (*si shi* 四 時) and five phases (*wu xing* 五 行) for giving life, growth, limit, and storage, and to produce cold, heat, dryness, damp and wind. Human beings have five *zang*, and through transformation, five *qi* to produce elation, anger, sadness, oppression and fear.'[118]

An 'emotion' (*qing* 情) is a movement of *qi* which affects the heart/mind, and which may also be linked with the other *zang* according to the resonances of the five elements/phases (*wu xing* 五 行). The character translated as emotion (*qing* 情) is made with the heart (忄) on the left, and the green colour associated with the vibrancy of life (青) on the right. The heart (心) is found within the construction of most of the characters for the individual emotions, and emotions are the natural activity and expression of the heart/mind. If they are able to flow through the heart quite freely, without attaching, then the heart/mind will be healthy. But emotions which are held in the heart, or attach to patterns within the mind, disturb and distort the natural *qi* patterning. This distortion will eventually affect the functioning of the *zang* – in the same way that a

---

118 The Rhythm at the Heart of the World, p. 23

distortion within the *qi* patterning of the *zang* may have an emotional effect.

The classical medical texts therefore regard human emotion as a cause of disease. The seasonal climates of cold, heat, dryness, damp and wind listed in Suwen chapter 5, are the external causes of disease, whereas joy, anger, sadness, oppression and fear are the causes of disease which come from within. Each emotion has a specific effect on the *qi*, which in turn may influence the internal functioning of the body. Any text on Chinese medicine will include discussion on the emotional or inner causes of disease. This is not always elaborated within modern Chinese books, but it is certainly understood.

In the classical texts, the emotions are often likened to the wind, they can be like a gentle breeze or a hurricane, soothing or spreading havoc. But the texts also suggest that if we are rooted in our own true nature (*xing* 性), then emotions will flow through us like the wind through a well rooted tree. The leaves may be disturbed, and even the branches may sway, but the tree will remain solid and upright. This is a common analogy, which also reflects the image of the spirits as birds, which will rest in a tree which is still. As the wind disturbs the leaves of the tree, so emotional disturbance affects the heart and can therefore scatter the spirits.

It is interesting to note the similarity between the characters *qing* (情) and *xing* (性) – and their alliteration is also no coincidence. *Xing* (性) is made with the heart radical (*xin* 忄) and to give life (*sheng* 生) – *qing* (情) also has the heart radical and the character for life, with the addition of *dan* (丹 of *dan tian* 丹田 – the cinnabar field or field of transformation).[119] Emotion is seen to effect change within the true nature, it is an alteration,

---

119 Wieger's Chinese Characters, Lesson 115 D

which may be fleeting and leave no trace but which may also mould the heart/mind, in a negative or positive way. The way we respond to our life experiences moulds our nature. Our emotional reactions create patterns which may be hard to break.

All emotions affect the equilibrium of the heart/mind, though within the medical texts each of the five *zang* is associated with a specific emotion. These relationships are described clearly in Suwen chapter 5, as mentioned within the study of the five *zang*. Here, joy or elation are related to the heart, fear with the kidneys, oppression with the lungs, anger with the liver and obsessive thought with the spleen. When associated with the five *zang*, and therefore the five elements, each emotion is seen to cause a disturbance within the *qi* pattern which reflects the movement of the related element: joy allows the *qi* to rise and expand, following the movement of fire; fear makes the *qi* descend, following the movement of water; anger creates a forceful upward and outward movement of *qi*, following the movement of wood; oppression or sadness contracts the *qi*, following the movement of metal, and obsessive thought goes round and round until the *qi* is tied in knots, following the movement of the earth. This is presented in a similar way in Suwen chapter 39:

> 'When there is anger (*nu* 怒) the *qi* rises up (*shang* 上)
> When there is elation (*xi* 喜) the *qi* becomes loose (*huan* 緩)
> When there is sadness (*bei* 悲) the *qi* disappears (*xiao* 消)
> When there is fear (*kong* 恐) the *qi* descends (*xia* 下)…
> When there is fright (*jing* 驚) the *qi* is in disorder (*luan* 亂)…
> When there is obsessive thought (*si* 思) the *qi* is knotted (*jie* 結).'[120]

---

120 The Seven Emotions, p. 53

Texts that specifically relate the emotions to the five elements or the five *zang* list five emotions, though the emotions mentioned may change slightly from text to text – other texts list six (as we see above) and others seven, a number which is often given to the totality of the emotions – the *qi qing* (七情), or seven emotions being a common phrase to describe all emotional patterns. '*Xi nu*' (喜怒 elation and anger) is a phrase also used to denote emotion in general, as in Huainanzi chapter 7:

> 'Heaven has wind and rain, cold and heat; human beings have taking and giving, joy and anger (*xi nu* 喜怒).'[121]

And again in Suwen chapter 5:

> 'Elation and anger (*xi nu* 喜怒) injure the *qi*
> Cold and heat injure the bodily form'[122]

Here elation and anger infer all human emotion, cold and heat all external climatic influences. And whereas the climates have a direct effect on the body, the emotions injure the *qi*. Each emotion has a specific effect on the *qi* and the way we deal with our emotions is seen to be of primary importance for the maintenance of health. If the emotions are fleeting, so is the effect. But if the same emotion is habitual or if one gets stuck in a specific emotional response, the *qi* pattern will be distorted, and each particular distortion may lead to a specific disturbance amongst the five *zang*. Looking more closely at each of the emotions, we will see more clearly what these specific effects may be.

---

121 Jing Shen; Huainanzi Chapter 7, p. 11
122 Rhythm at the Heart of the World, p. 23

ANGER: NU

The character *nu* (怒) is often used in classical texts to express an upward surge of *qi*, a release of something that has been held or pent up inside. Within the realm of the emotions it is translated as anger, and represents a powerful surge of emotional energy. The character may be found in other contexts in relation to the rising of energy at springtime – the stirring of life after the winter, and particularly as the force necessary to break open the seed and pierce the ground which allows the proliferation of growth to follow. We have seen this idea in association with the strength of the young *yang*, and also in the wood element and the associated effect of the liver *qi*, with its ability to spread upwards and to cut through stagnation. Anger is seen to have a similar rousing and arousing effect on the *qi*. So an aspect of what may be translated as anger is simply the natural impetus of life – and as with all the emotions, it is only when it is out of balance – either too strong or repressed – that it may be considered pathological.

We have seen that the tendency of the liver *qi* to rise is regulated by a rooting in the liver *yin* and blood, and by extension, the water of the kidneys. The wood element always needs its roots to be well nourished by water. In the same way, the emotion of anger is tempered by a rooting of the psyche. If the kidney *yin* is unable to nourish the liver blood, there may be irritability or sudden outbursts of anger. Heat or excess conditions of the liver may produce sudden violent anger or even rage, or if the inner cause persists, there may be a state of constant anger and irritability. Alcohol, which heats the liver and damages the capacity of the liver to hold the blood, is seen to have this kind of dramatic effect on the psyche, especially when there is long term use and physical liver damage.

In clinical practice, however, it is often the effects of repressed anger that are apparent in the *qi* pattern. This may literally be a repression of the life force or a restriction to the unfolding of the life destiny, which may happen for many reasons. We may repress what we really want to do in life because of a sense of duty, or a lack of security or simply circumstance. Here it may be necessary to see clearly what we are able to change and what we need to accept – without resentment.

As a natural assertion of the life force, anger may be associated with the right of the individual to be alive – and is often expressed in defence of one's sense of freedom and justice. In many cases, this expression of anger may be justified – but it may also be dangerous. The anger expressed in various kinds of social uprising often represents a reaction to the denial of human rights, or of individual freedom, where one may feel forced to live according to the standards or rules of others.

Here there is also a difference in attitudes towards freedom and self-expression between Eastern and Western cultures. The Western insistence on individual freedom and individual human rights is often superseded in Eastern cultures by concern for harmony in the society in general. The ability to assert one's self without neglecting the thoughts and feelings of others is expressed within the Confucian virtue associated with the wood element, *ren* (仁), benevolence or human kindness. It is in learning how to feel for others, to communicate with others, learning to give and take, that the emotions of anger and resentment are balanced. This has such an interesting application to all areas of human life – it addresses the questions that arise in our dealings with the individual in relation to society, how much to assert our individuality, how much to be a part of the group and of society at large. How do we balance that within our lives?

The Confucian virtues are used as a guide for human beings to live within society while remaining true to themselves; the virtues, and their embodiment in Confucian rites and rituals, enable expression of emotion, while providing a kind of social etiquette. But taken too far, or out of context, this could easily become a rigid control system.

In Chinese medical pathology, great or violent anger (*da nu* 大怒) forces the blood and *qi* upwards, reddening the face and eyes. In extremes it may cause vomiting of blood, and possibly cerebral vascular accidents. This is seen in Suwen chapter 3:

> 'The *yang qi*, prey to violent anger (*da nu* 大怒) …carry the blood to the top of the body, causing weakness through pressure.'[123]

Fury, or furious madness (*kuang nu* 狂怒) is a state closer to mania, but specifically a mania which comes from an uncontrollable long-term anger, which is often accompanied by random shouting. The left part of the character *kuang* (狂) depicts a mad dog. It suggests a permanent violent fury in which reason is completely lost. There may be a lack of awareness of those around. In Suwen chapter 46, Huangdi asks his physician Qi Bo about the nature of furious madness (*kuang nu* 狂怒), Qi Bo replies:

> 'The *yang qi* provokes abrupt violence, there is difficulty in decision and judgement, which brings about anger.'[124]

---

123 The Seven Emotions, p. 75
124 ibid. p. 76

And also in Lingshu chapter 8:

> 'In a state of swelling anger, one is disturbed and led astray. Everything is out of control.'[125]

A common example of irritability or anger is premenstrual tension, which relates to the function of the liver in both storing and releasing blood. Its manifestation will differ according to the patterns and tendencies of the individual – a full condition more likely to give rise to an expression of anger, while in cases of depletion there may be irritability. But according to the classical texts, if the woman is of a *yin* disposition, and unable to express anger directly, the blockage of the liver *qi* will tend to cause jealousy and suspicion.[126] Premenstrual tension provides an interesting example of how a blockage within the *qi* and blood may cause an emotional reaction; but it is also important to assess whether an underlying state of suppressed anger is creating a blockage of the *qi*. Always both scenarios are possible and very often one can no longer be disentangled from the other.

Nu (怒) is also mentioned in the classical texts as an anger which combines with an uncontrollable sexual desire. The arousal of the liver *qi* can be seen in conjunction with sexual arousal, usually in relation to the healthy ability to create and procreate. The liver and the wood element command the muscles and also the ability to sustain an erection. But this particular emotional state may be accompanied by a feeling of hatred towards the opposite sex, and therefore of a particular kind of domination and possibly violence.

---

125 Larre, C. and Rochat, E., Rooted in Spirit, Station Hill Press, 1995, p. 97

126 The Essential Woman, Monkey Press, 2007, p. 15, 35, 78

In each of these cases, a study of the movement of *qi*, combined with the resonances of the associated *zang*, and the quality of emotion, provides a rich ground for the understanding of emotional states, and a very practical and effective way to work with their associated behaviours and pathologies.

ELATION AND JOY: XI LE

The characters *xi* (喜) and *le* (樂) may both be translated as joy – but in order to differentiate their meaning, we tend to use the terms elation and joy respectively. *Xi* may also be translated as excitement, or over-excitement. The two characters are often used together to describe the emotional state connected to the heart and the fire element, but while both express an upward and expansive movement of the *qi* – *xi* has a more intense *yang* quality, while *le* suggests a more quiet, gently expansive, inner state of joy. The character *le* (樂), can also be pronounced *yue*, in which case it has the meaning of music.

Both characters have a relationship with music, and in particular with drums. The character *xi* (喜) represents the kind of music and singing heard at popular festivals, where the beating of a hand drum encourages dancing and excitement; the character *le* depicts a ceremonial drum with various gongs and chimes, which is used to give the correct measure and timing to certain rites and court rituals.[127] The etymology of the two characters describes well the difference between these contrasting aspects of joy.

Le (樂) expresses the natural joy of being alive; a feeling of connection and connectedness with all things. It is the kind of joy that wells up spontaneously as a reaction to a sunset, a rainbow, another human being. It must be close to our idea of love. To be without joy is maybe to be without love. Its pathological state is *bu le* (不 樂) lack of joy. *Bu le* (不 樂) is often seen in the philosophical texts as the result of going against the natural order of life – or against one's true nature, which will result in a lack of joy.

Xi (喜) is excitement. A *yang* movement which is somewhat similar to the impulse of life expressed in the character *nu* (怒); but this is joy not anger, and one is more likely to embrace other human beings than shout at them! It is a surge from the heart which expands and encompasses all around. Suwen chapter 39 says that elation loosens the *qi*, but can joy be a pathology? It depends on the situation and on the circumstance. Joy is not good and anger bad. But sometimes anger is an appropriate reaction, and joy inappropriate. A certain amount of loosening helps to get rid of tension in the body and distortions in the *qi* patterning, but too much and the *qi* is dissipated and scattered, as we see in the text of Lingshu chapter 8:

'When there is elation and joy (*xi le* 喜 樂), the spirits are scared away

---

127 The Seven Emotions, p. 96

and dispersed; there is no longer an ability to store.' [128]

Within the philosophical texts, overexcitement is certainly considered to be dangerous, it makes the blood race and disturbs the spirits. We can cope with a certain amount of excitement, but partying every night would loosen and scatter the *qi*. This could lead to exhaustion, but also an inability to be still. There may be a constant craving for stimulation.

These various states of the heart/mind are reflected in the use and abuse of mind altering drugs; whether stimulants or sedatives, mind expanding or narcotic, many drugs facilitate our ability to relate to others, to be sociable, to cope with our pain. The craving for excitement or a deep lack of joy may lead to a dependence on artificial stimulants, which inevitably take us further away from the natural experience of joy in our lives. Both ecstasy and LSD were originally used by psychologists to help those who felt locked inside themselves to relate to others. They were seen to bring a sense of connectedness where there had previously been alienation. Many other psychotropic substances have been traditionally used in ritual to enhance the connection with spirit, but they were carefully monitored by priests and shamans who understood their chemical actions. Today, very little is understood, even about the actions of prescribed drugs.

If the heart is constantly agitated or overstimulated, it may be unable to reflect reality. The heart/mind is likened to a mirror, or a pool of water, which if still and calm, gives a clear and accurate reflection of life. If the surface is unclear, agitated, the mind will be unclear, unable to distinguish between what is real and what is imaginary. There may even be visions and hallucinations.

The sound of laughter is associated with excitement and the fire

---

128 Rooted in Spirit, p. 93

element. Laughter frees up the *qi*, but uncontrollable or inappropriate laughter is a sign that the heart/mind is disturbed.

The character *kuang* (狂) which we saw previously as *kuang nu* (狂 怒), is also seen in the context of heart and fire pathology. Here it is simply madness. The texts suggest that this kind of heart pathology may be accompanied by silent laughter. Laughter is the natural response to the stimulation of the heart *qi*, but if the heart *qi* is exhausted, there is laughter with no sound. The character *dian* (癲) is used to describe another kind of madness, which often begins with a lack of joy, as we see in Lingshu chapter 22:

> 'First the patient is without joy. Then the head is heavy and painful and the eyes turn upwards and are red. When the disease becomes more serious …there is agitation and a feeling of unease in the chest area.'[129]

Joy is the natural condition for human beings – the joy of being alive, in tune with nature and with one's own nature. In this state the heart/mind is clear, and able to reflect reality; judgement is acute, decisions can be made. Daoist literature suggests that desires lead away from the ability to feel joy – until eventually nothing is enough. We begin to believe that happiness is dependent on what we have instead of who we are. Many daoist practices aim to lead us back to the stillness of the heart/mind, and a natural sense of joy.

---

129 The Seven Emotions, p. 105

FEAR: KONG

Fear is associated with the water element and has a descending action on the *qi*. The kidneys represent the foundation, the stability, the ability to hold – and to hold on. This is our survival instinct – it draws in and conserves. Fear may be a healthy reaction to a situation which threatens survival, or a pathological withdrawal and inability to engage with life. A firm psychological base in the kidney *qi* implies a trust in life. Its pathology often manifests as insecurity.

The character *kong* (恐) represents a hammer beating against the heart, and many of the classical descriptions of fear include fright, anxiety and apprehension – or a timidity which suggests a lack of foundation and an inability to trust.

> 'When there is fear and apprehension (*kong ju* 恐 懼) the spirits are agitated and scared away; nothing can be contained.'[130]

The character *ju* (懼), translated here as apprehension, represents a small bird, which is nervously on the look out for danger. The meaning of the character is a kind of fright, which may also include tremors or shaking. This fear and apprehension has an effect on the spirits, reflecting the close relationship between the heart and the kidneys, the fire and the water. In Lingshu chapter 10, which gives the pathologies of the meridians, that of the *shao yin* (heart and kidney meridians) is described

---

130 Lingshu chapter 8 in Rooted in Spirit, p. 99

as anxiety and jumpiness, 'like a man about to be arrested'.[131] We will see this later with *jing* (驚), also translated as fright, which often reflects a lack of communication between the heart and the kidneys. In Lingshu 8 above, the emotion linked to the kidneys has an effect upon the spirits. 'Nothing can be contained' suggests a leaking away of essences and *qi*, and possibly fluids.

Another expression, *chu ti* (怵 惕), is also found in Lingshu chapter 8, with the meaning of apprehension and anxiety:

> 'When there is apprehension and anxiety (*chu ti* 怵 惕), worry and preoccupation attack the spirits.'[132]

Here we see the pathology of the water element close to that of the earth – anxiety and apprehension being a mixture of fear, timidity and the obsessive thinking associated with the spleen.

A full blown fear, when one is in immediate danger for one's life – like coming across a tiger on our way home from work – is not something we tend to experience in modern industrialized society, but many people do experience a more or less constant low level anxiety, sometimes accompanied by apprehension. Fear stimulates a reaction in the adrenal glands which release adrenalin, producing the so-called fight or flight reaction. This is a good thing for running away from tigers. Maybe we have all experienced those superhuman feats that are somehow possible with a rush of adrenalin. The extra adrenalin in the bloodstream causes the heart to beat faster and the blood vessels to constrict; the result is more blood flow to the muscles and more oxygen to the lungs. The body

---

[131] The Seven Emotions, p. 84

[132] Lingshu chapter 8 in Rooted in Spirit, p. 82

could not cope with this state for long, but this kind of fear is generally short-lived, and the body soon recoups and returns to normal.

But exposure to noise, traffic, crowds, and general city living – which might include scary movies and video games – creates a chronic state of anxiety and tension. The body often maintains a low-level fight or flight state, which is not helped by the kind of advertising which stresses the insecurities of life and instils fear for our future well-being. Whether aware or not of the psychologically harmful effects, insurance companies, drug companies, government agencies of all kinds prey on insecurities to sell either products or doctrines in the guise of keeping us safe; using our anxieties to manipulate. It is not easy to keep an attitude of trust in life in this kind of environment, as trust is so easily undermined by constant exposure to negative messaging. These constant low-level fears weaken the kidney *qi*.

Here, in Lingshu 8, this apprehension and anxiety leads to a state of worry and concern, which affects the heart and the spirits. Weakness of kidney *qi* affects the spleen, and worry and preoccupation, generally a pathology linked with the spleen, is a result of this long-term decline of the kidneys which ultimately affects the spirits. The relationship between the kidneys, spleen and heart is compromised. If the base in the kidneys is not strong, all the *zang* may be ultimately affected.

In the pathology of fear, there often seems to be a break in the axis of communication between the kidneys and the heart, the *jing* (精 vital essences) and the *shen* (神 spirits). Suwen chapter 39 gives another example, though here it is the upper and lower heaters which are mentioned.

'When there is fear (*kong* 恐), the *qi* descends. When there is fear, the essences withdraw. Withdrawing, the upper heater is closed; the *qi* leaves. The lower heater becomes swollen; the *qi* does not circulate.'¹³³

The relationship between the kidneys and heart, the upper and lower heater, the water and fire aspect of the kidneys are all indicated here; there is a loss of communication and circulation. The fluids in the lower heater are no longer transformed by the fire of the triple heater, causing swelling and lack of circulation. There is often a pronounced retention of fluids in the abdomen and thighs. Later in Lingshu chapter 8 the pathology reflects the descending action of water:

'Under the effect of fear and fright (*kong ju* 恐 懼) from which one cannot free oneself, the essences are attacked; the bones grow stiff, there is impotence and withdrawal. At times the essences descend by themselves.'¹³⁴

This is a deep pathology, where the fear has damaged the kidney *qi* to the extent that the downward movement is causing seminal emissions. This same excessive downward movement of *qi* is seen in a lessening of the ability to retain or transform fluids. The attack on the essences affects the marrow and the bones – the bones become stiff through lack of nourishment. The result is a gradual seizing up and withdrawal.

The dynamic interactions between fire and water are seen clearly in the psychology of the heart and kidneys, and these kidney pathologies that result from fear reflect a lack of the warming and transforming power of fire. Fear is often the sign of a lack of trust in life, a deviation from our true nature and a loss of the joy of being alive. Fire and water must always

---

133 ibid. p. 81

134 Rooted in Spirit, p. 110

balance each other; the tendency of the heart fire towards excitement and over-exuberance is naturally tempered by the caution of the kidneys. The constant movement between heart and kidneys, spirits and essences, joy and fear, is what develops the virtue of the water element – wisdom. This is a practical wisdom, which is simply the know-how of living. It is by facing our fears, by shining the light of the heart/mind into our deepest inner spaces, that we become wise. As with all the processes between the heart and the kidneys, the *jing* and the *shen*, there is a kind of alchemy which results in an inner transformation.

THINKING: SI

Si (思) is simply to think. The character shows the heart (心) and above that, a primitive representation of the brain (田).¹³⁵ It indicates the communication between the heart and the brain which allows for the formation of impressions and ideas.

In Suwen chapter 5, thinking (*si* 思) is the emotion associated with the spleen and the earth element. The natural movement of the earth is rotation, and in this rotation the earth element aids movement from one stage to another, it unites and harmonizes the four seasons, the five phases, the five *zang*, the five tastes. In psychological terms, this rotation is the ability to turn things around in the mind. As the earth receives seeds

---

135 The Seven Emotions, p. 136

and enables them to grow, and the spleen receives the essences of food for nourishment of the body, so the mind receives thoughts and ideas – turning them around, assessing their value, digesting what is useful, rejecting what is not. And much as the spleen controls the sense of taste and is able to distinguish what food is good for us and what is not, the earth element facilitates the same kind of discrimination within the thinking processes. Some ideas are good for us, some maybe not so good.

The Confucian virtue associated with the earth element is honesty or integrity (*xin*, 信), translated variously as sincerity, faithfulness, truth. And maybe it is our honesty and integrity that provides the correct protection against the thoughts and feelings of others which may do us harm, acting as a filtering or sensing mechanism; we are able to discern what is in alignment with our own true nature and what is a deviation or diversion.

The 'worry and preoccupation' which we saw in the previous section is a translation of *si lü* (思 慮) – though in an earlier section of this same text, Lingshu chapter 8, *si lü* is simply translated as thought and reflection. So, in their non-pathological state, the characters suggest a process of turning things around in the mind, but if this process becomes stuck, it may become worries and concerns, overthinking or obsessive thought, as is stated in Suwen chapter 39:

'When there is obsessive thought (*si* 思) the *qi* is knotted (*jie* 結).'

The compulsive turning things around in the mind causes a knotting of the *qi* in the middle *jiao*, which may affect the digestion, but also hampers communication between the heart and the kidneys – the increased state of anxiety causing disruption along the water/earth/fire axis. A feeling of butterflies in the tummy – or of a pressure moving up against the heart are common descriptions of this kind of blockage or knotting in the *qi*.

Suwen chapter 8 states that the liver is in charge of 'the conception of plans' – and thinking needs to progress from a turning things around in the mind into some kind of action. The energy of the wood helps to move through this knotting of *qi*, and righteous anger can act as a motivator! A good balance between wood/earth is vital to healthy thought processes. The rumination of the earth tempers the impulse of the wood, and the movement of wood can give necessary direction to obsessive thinking. Strengthening the wood may encourage the *qi* to move out of this kind of earth impasse – though if the *qi* is blocked, it is advisable to take care when stimulating the wood, and make sure there is a firm grounding in the kidneys. Otherwise there may be a violent reaction.

We have seen in Lingshu chapter 8 that apprehension and anxiety lead to worries and concerns, and further in the paragraph there is a description of how this may lead to emaciation of the body form:

> 'Well developed forms become emaciated, the bulk of the flesh is ravaged.'[136]

Worries and concerns affect the appetite and also the ability to assimilate nourishment. A disruption in the spleen *qi* will always ultimately affect the body form. Eating disorders may have various causes, but whether one eats too much or too little, the natural tendency to nourish oneself is lost, and one is unable to accurately reflect body image. The heart and brain are not in correct communication, and there is an inability to reflect reality and to think clearly.

---

136 ibid. p. 150

SADNESS AND OPPRESSION: BEI YOU

Several characters may be translated as sadness and grief. In the character *bei* (悲) the heart is below (心) and above is *fei* (非) which is a negation, a denial, a negative prefix. It is literally a negation of the heart. It is usually translated as sadness, and suggests a movement of repression and restriction which is often associated with the metal element and the lungs. But in Suwen chapter 5 the expression of will associated with the metal element is *you* (憂), which may be translated as oppression or sometimes oppressive grief. The character *ai* (哀) is also often paired with *bei* (悲) and both characters are then translated as grief or mourning.

Different characters are used in different contexts to express the emotions of sadness, grief and oppression, but it is the same movement of constriction and pressure which is common to the metal element and to the *qi* in the autumn time. The relationship of sadness and oppression to the autumn is found in many cultures which share the seasons of the temperate northern hemisphere. In Europe, autumn is traditionally associated with the melancholic temperament – poetic, withdrawn and introspective. In Japan, the autumn is favoured as a time of particular beauty – the traditional society venerating its soft colours, obscuring mists, its sense of loss and things that are not quite seen.

In the medical texts, sadness and grief affect the lungs. Pressure and constriction cause the chest to collapse, the breath to become short – it is no longer possible to take a deep breath and the kidneys and lungs begin to lose their proper exchange and interrelationship.

In Lingshu chapter 8, sadness and grief, sorrow and oppression, are seen to have a slightly different effect on the *qi*:

> 'In sadness and grief (*bei ai* 悲 哀) one is moved at the very centre, used up and exhausted, and the generation of life is lost… In sorrow and oppression (*chou you* 愁 憂), the *qi* is closed and blocked, and there is no circulation (行).'[137]

Both suggest a closing in and a closing down – *bei ai* (悲 哀) giving a more acute vision of grief and mourning. *Chou* (愁), translated above as sorrow, is made with the character for the autumn (秋) placed over the heart (心). Literally, autumn in the heart. Autumn is the time for letting go – grief and sadness the natural reaction to this loss.

In modern life, we often do not give ourselves the time to grieve. We no longer have rites and rituals that help us through times of loss – and society expects us just to carry on. Not so long ago we wore black arm bands when someone in the family died, so that everyone would know to treat us with special care. There would be a prescribed time when this was necessary, followed by stages of return to normality. In Eastern cultures, there are special days for tending the family graves, but we no longer seem to visit the graves of our ancestors. These simple rituals allow a space for grief. They give it shape and form. To light a candle on a death day is a small act which gives our sadness a place.

The autumn reminds us that life is constant change and transformation,

---

137 ibid. p. 113, 132

and that it is not possible to hold on to the past. As the trees shed leaves and plants die back, we are reminded that to allow new growth, the old must go. The scales, which appear as a symbol for the autumn in both China and the West (as in the scales of the zodiac sign Libra) allow us to judge and weigh up what we should keep and what we should let go of in order to move forward. The virtue associated with metal and the autumn is justice, which again is symbolized by the scales. Grief that is repressed often surfaces later in life in lung problems. In Suwen chapter 39 it simply says: 'When there is sadness (*bei* 悲), the *qi* disappears.'

In Suwen chapter 5 oppression (*you* 憂) is related specifically to the lungs, where it follows the movement of the metal element in its contraction and constriction, but it may also be seen affecting other *zang* and is sometimes coupled with other emotions. Its effect on the *qi* is one of blocking by pressure and restriction, and this can be seen very clearly, for example, where it is linked to the spleen in a later section of Lingshu chapter 8:

'When the spleen is prey to sorrow and oppression (*chou you* 愁 憂) and is not able to free itself, there is injury to the intent (*yi* 意). The intent being injured, one is in a state of complete disorder, the four limbs can no longer be raised…'[138]

Intent (*yi* 意) is related to the earth, and here we can see both the mental and physical effects of oppression on the spleen. Oppression affects the ability of the spleen to transport and transform. This manifests in an inability to nourish the body, and particularly the muscles. There is a kind of wastage, and the strength of the four limbs is diminished.

---

138 Rooted in Spirit, p. 116

THE EMOTIONS

FRIGHT: JING

We have already seen the characters *kong ju* (恐 懼) translated as fear and fright, where *ju* (懼) was described as a small bird always on the lookout for danger.[139] But another character which is commonly translated as fright is *jing* (驚). In Suwen chapter 39 *jing* is included in the list of emotions:

'When there is fright (*jing* 驚) the *qi* is in disorder (*luan* 亂)…'

The character *jing* (驚) has the horse radical at the bottom (馬), and above a kind of restraint (敬). Horses are fast and powerful, but also wilful and uncontrollable. In the character *jing* (驚) there is a suggestion of the tension between the horse and the attempt at restraint, and *jing* suggests a temperament that is highly strung and nervous. It is also to be startled – a kind of 'starting with fright' or jumpiness; there is a lack of ease, which may result in a physical jumping with fright or even tremors. As with *you* (憂), oppression, *jing* is not related to one specific element or *zang* – but more a relationship between the *zang* which is strained or even snapped. In particular, there may be a breaking of communication between the kidneys and the heart or the kidneys and the liver.

Jing refers to the kind of jumpiness where one may start at loud noises, even the ringing of the phone or the door bell; or the kind of

---

139 The Seven Emotions, p. 79

'light sleeper' who wakes at the slightest noise. There is a general lack of equilibrium in the body and mind. If the jumpiness is of a more physical nature, and seems to affect the muscles, this suggests a lack of kidney *yin* nourishing the liver blood. If the muscles are not properly nourished, there may be tremors, shaking, and even, in the extreme, convulsions.

In Suwen chapter 4, which introduces the resonances of the four seasons, and differs in some respects from the more well known five element resonances of Suwen chapter 5, we read that:

> 'The natural green colour of the eastern quarter penetrates and communicates with the liver; its orifice is the eye; its essences are stored in the liver …its disorder is shown in starting and jumpiness (*jing hai* 驚 駭).'[140]

If the jumpiness seems to be more a state of mind, there is a lack of communication between the heart and the kidneys – the essences are not able to attract and hold the spirits. Here there may be heart palpitations. We read further in Suwen chapter 39:

> 'When there is starting with fright (*jing* 驚) the heart no longer has a place to rely on, the spirits have no place to refer to, reflection (*lü* 盧) has no place to settle. This is how the *qi* is in disorder.'[141]

Whether the kidney/liver or kidney/heart relationship is affected, in both situations the kidneys are unable to provide a stable foundation.

---

140 ibid. p. 156

141 ibid. p. 55

THE FIVE ASPECTS OF SPIRIT: WU SHEN

We have seen within the classical literature that the *shen* (神), spirit or spirits, are the beneficial influences which flow down from heaven (*tian* 天). *Tian* may be translated as heaven but it always implies the natural order of things, and the way things constantly move, change and transform in order to retain that order. Within human beings, *shen* has a strong relationship with the concept of *xing* (性), the true nature, or the heavenly order reflected within us. As such, *shen* may be translated as spirit, intelligence, consciousness.

But within these early texts, we also come across the terms *hun po* (魂魄) and *yi zhi* (意 志) which make up the *wu shen* (五 神), or five aspects of spirit. As with *shen*, these terms are difficult to define, and have also been used with different meanings in different contexts throughout the centuries. Within medical literature, *hun* and *po* are often translated as ethereal soul and corporeal soul; in other non-medical texts they may be found within the context of ritual, and, in particular, funeral rites, where appropriate procedures are required to assure the correct movement of these souls after death. Here the *hun* are the heavenly souls, *po* the earthly souls, creating a *yin yang* couple within the ethereal realms.

Yi and *zhi* are aspects of human consciousness – the ways in which the mind and thought processes of an individual human being are formed. And in the same way that *hun* and *po* are often used together to express the nonphysical attributes of human life, so *yi* and *zhi* are used together to express the functioning of human consciousness. They are usually translated as intent and will.

While Chinese philosophers might have understood spirit as an aspect of human consciousness, at the same time there was a belief in the spirits of rocks and mountains, and an understanding of the importance of revering the spirits of ancestors. These different perspectives existed, and probably still exist, happily together.

Academics researching these different approaches within Chinese culture have often made distinctions between, for example, philosophical Daoism and religious Daoism; philosophy on the one hand dealing with the highly intellectual and acceptable process of understanding the world and our place within it, religious Daoism on the other as simple peasant superstition. But these two strands intertwine and coexist, as is the case within most cultures: there tends to be a more philosophical path which accepts personal responsibility for life, another which turns to the external – whether to a priest or a shaman, or simply by praying to an external deity – as a source of help or solace. All of this tends to exist together, and becomes part of the complex understanding of spirit. Confucius suggested that it is possible to deal respectfully with the spirits while keeping a distance;[142] and that it is our responsibility to moderate our own behaviour, and not to look to external causes for our good or bad fortune.

So the development of a philosophy of consciousness did not replace the idea of the spirits, but within both Confucianism and Daoism there is an attempt to understand that it is our destiny as human beings to create the right environment for a kind of spiritual illumination (*shen ming* 神) to manifest itself.

---

142 Lunyu chapter 6 in Aspects of Spirit, Monkey Press 2013, p. 72

The text of Lingshu chapter 8 gives a step by step account of the formation of an individual human life, and is a key text for the understanding of these subtle aspects of human consciousness. At the beginning of the chapter, the emperor, Huangdi, asks his physician, Qi Bo, a question regarding the origin of a state of complete disorder, possibly madness; he wants to know whether it is the fault of heaven (nature) or of the individual. He then goes on to ask:

'And what is the meaning of *de* (德 virtue), *qi* (氣), *sheng* (生 life), *jing* (精 essences), *shen* (神), *hun* (魂), *po* (魄), *xin* (心 heart/mind), *yi* (意 intent), *zhi* (志 will), *si* (思 thought), *lü* (慮 reflection), *zhi* (知 wisdom)?

'Qi Bo replies: Heaven in me is virtue, earth in me is *qi*. Virtue flows, *qi* spreads out and there is life. When two essences embrace, that is called the spirits; that which faithfully follows the spirits in their coming and going is called the *hun* (魂); that which associates with the essences in their entries and exits, is called the *po* (魄). That which takes charge of the being is called the heart/mind (*xin* 心). When the heart/mind is applied, that is called intent (*yi* 意); when intent is permanent, that is called will (*zhi* 志). When will is maintained but also changes, that is called thought (*si* 思); when thought spreads far and powerfully that is called reflection (*lü* 慮), when reflection is actualized, that is called wisdom (*zhi* 知). Wisdom is nothing other than the ability to nourish life (*yang sheng* 養 生).'[143]

Qi Bo's answer is beautifully constructed; the structure and poetry of the classical Chinese in his account of the process of the generation and

---

143 The Heart in Lingshu chapter 8

development of life and consciousness, make it one of the most highly regarded texts within the Neijing.[144]

The answer begins, 'heaven in me is virtue' – but virtue is a difficult word in a Western context as it has come to imply a kind of morality which is not present in the Chinese. Other translators choose to translate *de* (德) as power, which also has limitations. *De* is the manifestation of the *dao* within beings and things. The *dao* in me is virtue, or power – it is *dao* in action. As this manifestation of the *dao* flows to earth, there is *qi*; as *qi* spreads there is life. The embrace of two essences, which here suggests the essence of a man and a woman, summons the spirits. The *hun* follow the *shen* to become that aspect of spirit which is individual to each being; the *po* follow the essences, bringing vitality to the physical form. Then comes the heart/mind which takes charge of the individual being. The heart/mind is the capacity within human beings for self-consciousness, and will and intent are the first formations within the mind which lead to thought, reflection, and ultimately wisdom – which is nothing other than the practical wisdom needed to nourish and maintain life in the correct and most efficient way.

And the correct and most efficient way is that the activity of consciousness is ruled by the heart; the *hun* follow the *shen*, the *po* follow the *jing*. The *jing shen* align with the manifestation of the *dao* – or heaven within me.

Within medical theory, the five *shen* (*wu shen* 五 神) are related to the five *zang*, and are often seen to reflect the more subtle aspects of the function of the *zang*. They follow the five phase correspondances and the *shen* is related to the heart, the *hun* to the liver, the *po* to the lungs,

---

144 The text is discussed in depth in The Heart in Lingshu chapter 8, which also gives the Chinese text.

the *yi* to the spleen and the *zhi* to the kidneys – though in certain texts, the kidneys are related to *jing* (vital essences) in this same context. As we look at the key terms, we will come back to this seminal text of Lingshu chapter 8, and its guidance for human life. The title of the chapter is *ben shen* (本 神), Rooted in Spirit.

SHEN

Within the medical texts, the spirits are specifically related to the heart. This is stated very clearly in Suwen chapter 9:

'The heart is the root of life, and the changes (*bian* 變) operated by the spirits.'[145]

The spirits require a peaceful heart that is not too disturbed by the emotions. The quiet or empty heart is likened to a still pool of water which gives a true reflection of its surroundings; or a mirror, the surface of which needs to be cleaned regularly in order to reflect back a true picture of reality. The information reflected by the heart is provided by the sense organs which are mediated by the heart and the brain. The brain is called the *yuan shen zhi fu*, 原 神 之 府, the *fu* of the original *shen*.

This philosophical approach to the spirits as aspects of consciousness

---

145 The Double Aspect of the Heart, p. 6

is generally quite acceptable to the Western mind, but the medical texts insist on a very direct relationship between the physical, mental and spiritual aspects of a human being. As we see in Lingshu chapter 8, the *shen* are stored (guarded, *cang* 藏) by the heart and within the circulation of blood and *qi* (*mai* 脈):

'The heart stores the *mai*; the *mai* are the dwelling place of the *shen*.'[146]

The spirits depend on the quality of the essences and the blood and bring consciousness not only through the heart/mind but throughout the whole body, via the *mai*. The *shen* within us manifest themselves in the other aspects of spirit.

HUN

Lingshu chapter 8 tells us that the *hun* follow the *shen* in their comings and goings. They are able to exist separately from the physical body, although in order for the body to function fully, the *hun* must be present. Daoist texts describe the *hun* as journeying both in dreams and in meditation, either under the conscious control of the individual, or unconsciously in sleep. Dreams may be seen as both illuminating or as pathological depending on their type and content. It is possible to travel

---

146 The Double Aspect of the Heart, p 32

in dreams, to meet other souls, to receive information and instruction, to experience sublime states of consciousness; but it is also possible to experience confused, disturbing states, which are simply a reflection of a disordered heart/mind. The Zhuangzi refers to the meeting of souls within dreams (chapter 2) but also describes them as an agitation of the soul, as in chapter 6 when it states that 'authentic men' sleep without dreams.

The ability of the *hun* to travel is both real and metaphysical, and the *hun* represent that part of the consciousness which is far reaching, visionary, imaginative – able to connect with the bigger picture. But the *hun* must be grounded, and in order to return safely to the body, require a solid basis within the *yin*. The *hun* are related to the liver and the wood element; they are able to travel far, to expand and fly, but they are attracted to the body by the *yin* of the liver. They make their home in the liver blood. Without a strong connection to the physical, the *hun* may wander and not return, which could mean death, or there may be a tenuous hold on physical reality – the individual being dreamy and ungrounded.

We see in Suwen chapter 9:

> 'The liver is the trunk of extreme cessation;
> it is the residence of the *hun* (魂)…'[147]

And in Lingshu chapter 8:

> 'The liver stores the blood; the blood is the dwelling place of the *hun*.'[148]

---

147 The Liver, p. 62
148 Rooted in Spirit, p. 141

The strange term 'extreme cessation' is close to the meaning of the *jue* (厥) of *jue yin* – the liver channel. It often relates to the end of one phase or state and the beginning of another. *Jue* is used to describe the dark moon – invisible, but the beginning of a new moon cycle; the ebb and flow of the tide. It is the moment that the tide changes. The liver is always both end and beginning – the extreme of *yin* before turning to *yang*. There is also a relationship between the *hun* and the *shao yang*:

'The *hun* (魂) are like clouds (*yun* 云), they are the *qi* of the young *yang* (*shao yang* 少 陽) and therefore move without stopping.'[149]

The character for *hun* (魂) is made with that of an earth spirit (*gui* 鬼) with the cloud radical (云) on the left. Both the *hun* (魂) and *po* (魄) share this earth spirit character – and although the *hun* are seen as *yang* in relation to the *po*, and to be more heavenly in nature, they are both aspects of spirit manifest within the earth (the body). The *hun* still have the ability to spread like clouds and move with the agility of the young *yang*, while the *po* remain earthbound. But whereas the *shen* are beyond definition by *yin* and *yang*, the *hun* and *po* are the *yin* and *yang* expression of spirit within a human being.

The relationship between the *hun* and the liver is reflected in the ability of the *hun* to move freely. They reflect the wood element in its movement of upward expansion, the wind in its comings and goings. They enable vision and the ability to envision a future.

---

149 Baihutong (Discussion of the White Tiger Hall) in Aspects of Spirit, p. 29

PO

In Lingshu chapter 8 the *po* 'associate with the essences in their entries and exits': they do not come and go freely like the *hun*, but need regulation, gates and doors. The *po* are the *yin* aspect of this earthly soul and cling to the essences. They do not leave the body, except on death, and then it is preferable that they leave slowly, decomposing back into the earth as the body itself returns to dust. Both the *hun* and *po* are served with specific rites at death; the *po* is sealed within the body by plugging the orifices with jade, if you are rich, with rice if you are poor. A *po* that escapes at death may still experience the physical desires of the body, and become a hungry ghost. The Far East abounds with stories of hauntings by hungry ghosts: souls who died in battle, or were murdered figuring large in the genre. These ghosts and spirits often do not know that they are dead – they may continue to hang around their usual haunts, unable to be still, led by desires of the body or emotional attachment.

It is still common for temples in both China and Japan, and much of East Asia, to leave offerings of food for hungry ghosts, and to conduct special rituals to guide them into a more peaceful state where they are able to let go of their pain or need for revenge, and to accept their death.

The Mawangdui funeral banner, excavated in the 1970s from a tomb dating back to the 2nd century BCE, is typical of the funeral imagery of the time. The banner was placed over the coffin of a woman of rank, and acts as a guide to her souls after her death. The banner depicts her three *hun* being guided to heaven, her seven *po*, offered food, and guided into the underworld. (See Fig. 11)

Fig. 11: The Mawangdui funeral banner. In the centre the woman is depicted with her three hun behind her. Below, the seven po are given offerings of food and wine before they descend to the underworld.

In life, the *hun* and *po* must remain together, in death, they separate, and, according to their nature, the *hun* rise to heaven to become one with the *shen*, the *po* decompose with the essences back into the earth. In the Liji, the Book of Rites:

'The *hun* and the *qi* return to heaven; the body form (*xing* 形) and the *po* return to the earth.'[150]

The *po* are the basic physical drive of life; they keep the body functioning at an unconscious level – the beating of the heart, the movement along the digestive tract; absorption and assimilation; it is the primal drive to live and to survive. At birth, the first breath engages that instinctual force of life – and the breath continues to mediate deep body functioning giving it rhythm and continuity. We see in Suwen chapter 9:

'The lung is the trunk in which the *qi* is rooted; it is the dwelling place of the *po*.'[151]

And in Lingshu chapter 8:

'The lungs store the *qi*; the *qi* are the dwelling place of the *po*.'[152]

As blood, with its *yin* nature, is able to act as a holding place for the *hun*, which like to drift away, the *qi* is the residence of the *po* – helping them to circulate and ascend, giving to the *po* their ability to be present

---

150 Aspects of Spirit, p. 17
151 The Lung, p. 46
152 Aspects of Spirit, p. 42

throughout the whole body, while the rhythmic breathing of the lungs maintains the involuntary responses within the organism. The *po* rule those deep regulations, the parts of our life which go on without our consciousness – if the *hun* are away, then the *po* maintain the body in a kind of coma state until the *hun* return. There is no consciousness, but there is still life. The autonomic nervous system may be the closest we can come to a description of the function of the *po* in Western medicine. It is a kind of instinctive and cellular intelligence, which nevertheless responds to the breath.

The character for *po* (魄) is made with *gui* (鬼) and white (*bai* 白). This whiteness relates to the metal element, to the autumn and the descending movement, but also to death and the bones within the earth, symbolizing the return.

YI

The *yi* (意) follows the heart/mind in the text of Lingshu chapter 8. The character is made with a sound or musical note (*yin* 音) over the heart (心). *Yin* is used to describe the five tones which are associated with the five elements, and the character *yi* suggests a resonance with the heart; or a sound which is modulated by the heart. As with the characters for the emotions, both *yi* and *zhi* contain the heart in their construction, and following the heart in the text, the characters emphasize that it is only once the heart has taken charge of the individual being that the *yi* and the *zhi* are able to manifest themselves.

Yi is the first formation of the mind, the beginning of directed thought. But it is also to remain in a state of awareness, without allowing the development of thinking. In this context, *yi* is commonly used in the martial arts and meditation to define the focus of the mind on a specific action, or possibly non-action. It is not concentration, but to be totally present and in the present moment, not allowing the mind to wander. It has the same meaning in clinical practice, where it is not to direct an outcome, but to be totally present with the situation, with the patient, with the moment.

Our awareness may be coloured by preconceptions, or by wants and desires; but here, with the first formation of thoughts, it is important to be aware of these patterns, and the way in which they direct our responses. This is all part of polishing the mirror of the mind in order to reflect a true picture of the world around us. Many of the Confucian texts advise nourishing the mind with good music, poetry, the words of the sages, and to examine the mind every day, to reflect on the desires and thinking. Through the *yi*, one is able to cultivate the heart/mind.

'The tendency of the heart/mind is what is known as the *yi*.'[153]

Yi and *zhi* are often used together to designate the inner disposition, or temperament, but within the specific categories of the *wu shen* (五 神), *yi* is related to the spleen, the earth element, and is generally translated as intent. This is seen later in chapter 8:

---

[153] Chunqiu Fanlu in Aspects of Spirit, p. 130

'The spleen stores the *ying* (營, nutrition, re-construction); the *ying* is the dwelling place of the *yi*.'[154]

We have seen that Suwen chapter 5 gives thought (*si* 思) as the 'aspect of will' expressed through the spleen and the earth element. *Yi* has a close affinity with thought, but it comes before the actual formation of thoughts and ideas. In medical terminology, the spleen offers the best of its essences to the heart, and must remain in close harmony with the heart. The *yi* nourishes the heart/mind, and has the ability to assess and evaluate what is presented to the mind in the form of thoughts and ideas.

Situated at the centre, the spleen and the earth maintain the relationship between heart and kidneys, *jing* and *shen* – and in Lingshu 8, the *yi* is placed between the heart/mind and the *zhi* (志), the will, which is associated with the kidneys. There is also an important connection between the focus of the mind, and the ability to be centred in oneself.

'When the spleen falls prey to oppression and sorrow, the *yi* (意) is attacked.'[155]

Emotional states cloud the ability of the *yi* to discern what should be presented to the heart; and an intent that is shaken may also affect the will. We have seen the continuation of this passage (pp. 70-71), where a lack of *yi* caused a weakness in the spleen and ultimately an inability to move the limbs.

---

154 Rooted in Spirit, p. 136

155 ibid. p.108

ZHI

When the intent (*yi* 意) is permanent or fixed, that is called will (*zhi* 志). The character *zhi* (志) is made with the heart and a character which depicts the emergence of a sprout through the earth. It is a powerful symbol of growth while also suggesting a firm rooting. Its most ancient use is as a symbol of fertility. *Zhi* refers to the fixing of the mind; to fix one's mind on a goal, and often in the philosophical texts, to fix one's mind on the *dao*, (*zhi yu dao* 志 於 道). But this fixing of the will must also be flexible, and to be fixed on the *dao* means that it is possible to change according to circumstances while remaining stable within one's natural disposition. It is not to remain fixed in a rigid way. The following line of Lingshu chapter 8 says that when the will is maintained, but is also able to change, then there is thought. So there needs to be stability, a rooting in the kidneys, but also flexibility.

We see again that in the medical texts the *yi* and *zhi* may refer generally to the inner disposition and functioning of the mind, or may specifically be related to the spleen and the kidneys. Lingshu chapter 8:

'The kidneys store the essences; the essences are the dwelling place of the will (*zhi* 志).'[156]

In its relationship with the kidneys and the essences, the *zhi* is close to

---

156 ibid. p. 136

the origins of life. It is the rooting of the heart/mind in the authenticity of the origin. The will is able to direct the *qi*, and Suwen chapter 2 explains that in each of the four seasons the will directs the *qi* in a specific way, in order to be in tune with the *qi* of the season; in the spring, exerting the will for life (*yi shi zhi sheng* 以 使 志 生); in summer, exerting the will without violence (*shi zhi wu nu* 使 志 無 怒); in autumn, exerting the will peacefully and calmly (*shi zhi an ning* 使 志 安 寧); and in winter, exerting the will as if buried, as if hidden (*shi zhi ruo fu ruo ni* 使 志 若 伏 若 匿).[157] This is part of the will's ability to adapt and change according to circumstance and to direct the *qi* according to the *qi* of the universe. Human behaviour is a direct result of the ability of the individual will to exert its influence.

In Suwen chapter 5 the character *zhi* is seen again as an 'expression of will' related to each of the five elements; the expression of will related to the wood is anger, to water, fear, etc. This suggests that each emotion is a way in which the will can be directed, and possibly misdirected, according to the movements of the five phases. If the will remains well rooted, the emotion will be a fleeting movement of *qi*; if the rooting of the will is disturbed by the emotion, it may cause an imbalance in the *qi*, and subsequent damage to the *zang*, as we see in Lingshu 8:

'When the kidneys are prey to a swelling anger, the will is injured. If the will is injured, one no longer remembers what one has just said. The lower back becomes stiff and one cannot bend forwards or backwards…'[158]

'When the lung falls prey to boundless elation and joy, the *po* are

---

157 The Way of Heaven

158 Rooted in Spirit, p. 110

attacked. The *po* being attacked, one becomes mad (*kuang* 狂). With madness, the intent (*yi* 意) knows no one. The skin shrivels and wrinkles…' [159]

The text of Lingshu 47 illustrates the way that these various spiritual aspects are understood within the more general view of the human body/mind complex:

> 'Human beings, having blood and *qi* (*xue qi* 血 氣), essences and spirits (*jing shen* 精 神), receive life from them and they ensure the regular movement between nature (*xing* 性) and destiny (*ming* 命). …Will and intent (*zhi yi* 志 意) are what direct the essences and spirits (*jing shen* 精 神), gather *hun* and *po* (魂 魄), regulate hot and cold, harmonize and blend elation and anger (*xi nu* 喜 怒)… When will and intent are in harmony, then the essences and spirits are concentrated and correct; *hun* and *po* are not dissipated, regret and anger do not arise, the five *zang* do not receive perverse influences. The five *zang* (臟) are for guarding (*cang* 藏) the essences and spirits, blood and *qi*, *hun* and *po*.' [160]

---

159 ibid. p. 110

160 Aspects of Spirit, p. 51

THE MERIDIAN NETWORK: JING MAI

Neijing Suwen chapter 5:

'The Emperor said: I was taught that the sages of ancient time presented the principles (*li* 理) organizing the human body; ordering and differentiating (*li bie* 列 別) the *zang* and the *fu*, determining the extremities and branchings of the meridian network (*luo jing mai* 絡 經 脈); grouping them together to ensure free communication in the six junctions (*liu he* 六 合), each according to its normal pattern (*jing* 經); assigning to each cavity of *qi* (*qi xue* 氣 穴 – acupuncture point) which springs from them a location and a name; recognizing how activity (*jin* 筋, muscular movement) arises from the ravines and valleys (of the flesh) and the bones which support them; giving to each well-divided region, with its currents and counter-currents, the principle of inner organization (*tiao li* 條 理); the *yin yang* of the four seasons giving it cyclical regulation (*jing ji* 經 紀); recognizing all the outward and inward (*wai nei* 外 內) exchanges in the correspondences of exterior and interior (*biao li* 表 裡).'[161]

After this extraordinary explanation of the structure and organization

---

161 The Rhythm at the Heart of the World, p. 27

of the human body, the Emperor asks the question: 'Can we really put our faith in that?'

So maybe there has always been speculation about what this network of connections may be. Certainly in modern times, the existence of the meridians of acupuncture has been challenged, and attempts are made to relate the effects of acupuncture to the nervous system and the possible stimulation of particular hormones within the brain. But although some specific relationships have been made with various aspects of nervous function, the meridians of Chinese medicine do not conform to any known pathways of transmission within Western medicine. As scientific understanding progresses and is able to define more clearly the subtle mechanisms of information transfer within the organism, maybe we will develop a more precise understanding of the nature of these pathways – an understanding which is likely to include a combination of many different functions.

It has been suggested that there may be an electrical transfer of information throughout the water-rich areas of the derma; that the hormones travelling through the blood stream carry chemical messages which inform physical and emotional change; that intelligence is not only within the brain, but throughout the whole body. There is much to be discovered and the ancient Chinese understanding may have some important ideas to offer in these areas of research.

But fundamental to an understanding of Chinese medicine, and particularly to acupuncture, massage and exercise therapies, is the acceptance of a network of very specific pathways within the body. These have often been called 'energy pathways' – but it has never been very clear what is meant by energy in this context. Most certainly within Chinese medicine this network of vessels would include the movement of blood and nutrients throughout the body, as well as more subtle or non-physical components, which we may call *qi* in its various expressions. Many excellent books are available which give a very thorough presentation of the channels and points of acupuncture; here the intention is to look at the classical literature in order to clarify how the ancient Chinese conceived of these pathways; to look at the differences in function of the various meridians, channels and their divergences, based on the meaning of the characters themselves, and descriptions of their functions within classical texts.

The three most common characters used to describe the meridian network are *jing* (經), *luo* (絡) and *mai* (脈). They are used both separately, when each term describes a distinct function, and in various combinations.

> 'The *jing mai* (經 脈) circulate (*xing* 行) blood and *qi*. They ensure the free communication of *yin* and *yang* so that the body can flourish.'[162]

Mai 脈 (脉)

Mai is a very general term which refers to the circulation of blood and *qi* throughout the organism. It is also the character used for the pulse – a pulsation of the blood and *qi* at a particular location on the body where this circulation may best be felt and assessed.

The character is formed with the phonetic *yong* (永) and the radical for the flesh, or a part of the body (肉 becoming 月). *Yong* is made up of the character for water (水), with two extra strokes at the top which signify

---

[162] Nanjing difficulty 23; Lecture notes, Jing Luo, 1999

duration. In modern Chinese, *yong* is to last or endure, to be constant. Its etymology suggests the flow of water, particularly within the ground. In Wieger's Chinese Characters, which is based on the 2nd century CE Shuowen Jiezi, it is everflowing, or everlasting: 'The unceasing flow of water veins within the earth'.[163] In the human body it suggests something that flows unceasingly and yet is hidden within.

Classical Chinese medical literature describes the body as a landscape; the flesh and muscles as mountains, valleys and ravines; the *mai* (脈) as the flow of water through the landscape – which includes wells, springs, streams, rivers and seas; marshes, ditches, ponds and gorges. It also implies the complete hydrological cycle, which includes the evaporation, condensation and perpetual movement which keeps the system circulating and constantly renewed. Acupuncture point names frequently reflect this vision of a water system. The first points of both the kidney and heart meridians, the two channels intimately connected to the source, are called springs; Heart 1, *ji quan* (極 泉), highest, or ultimate, spring; Kidney 1 *yong quan* (湧 泉), gushing spring. The main acupuncture points located between the toes and the knees, the finger tips and the elbows, are categorized as wells, springs, streams, rivers and seas, and as the water system of a river valley both forms and follows the structure of the land, so the *mai* are shaped by and shape the body.

Body therapists follow these hills and ravines, the so called 'divisions of the flesh' (*fen rou* 分 肉) and acupuncturists locate points by tracing its subtle terrain. With practice, it is possible to feel each cavity of *qi* (*qi xue* 氣 穴), just as Zhuangzi's butcher could feel the paths of least resistance for his knife.[164] The body has gaps and spaces, hollows and caverns. We

---

163 Wieger's Chinese Characters, Lesson 125 D/E

164 Zhuangzi chapter 3

become familiar with the landscape of the body, just as walking the paths on the earth brings familiarity with our environment. We get to know where to expect springs and streams, ponds and wells. We can feel stagnation and waterlogging, drought and erosion. The outer form tells us something of what is beneath the ground, or hidden within.

The *mai* represent this whole hydrological system – they are both the physical and non-physical aspects of circulation, the blood and the *qi*. And they are the places where this underground current can be felt at the surface – the pulse. The *mai* are related to the heart, which is responsible for the circulation of blood and *qi*. 'The heart masters the *mai* (*xin zhu mai* 心 主 脈)' is a common phrase found throughout the medical texts.

The rhythm of the heart, assisted by the lungs, gives impetus to the *mai*. This rhythm is felt at the pulse. The pulse is taken on the lung channel, which carries the first impulse of the *qi*, at the radial artery, where blood and *qi* pools into the Great Abyss (*tai yuan* 太 淵, Lung 9). Here the narrow channelling enables the practitioner to assess blood and *qi* in all their *yin/yang* variations.

Often translated within the medical literature as vessel, within the Monkey Press books, *mai* is generally translated as 'vital circulation' to capture its breadth of meaning.

Jing 經

The character *jing* (經) is made with the silk thread radical on the left, suggesting a threadlike continuity. The phonetic (巠), on the right, again shows streams of water flowing under the earth. But whereas the radical for the flesh within the *mai* character suggested a diffusion of streams throughout the body, the silk thread suggests a more precise regulation – and the character *jing* (經) is used in many different contexts to describe a form of organization and regulation. It is the term used for a meridian of longitude, reflecting the north-south, pole to pole axis of the earth. Similarly, it is the longitudinal threads, or the weft, of a weaving loom; the vertical threads which give the structure and correct tension for the cloth to be woven.

But *jing* (經) has other interesting meanings. It is the *jing* of the Daodejing (道 德 經), the Yijing (易 經), and the Neijing (內 經) – where the character suggests a transmission of information from heaven – a sacred text which gives guidance for life. Within classical texts, *jing* (經) is often seen with the meaning of the regulation bestowed by heaven, or the manifestation of the natural order.

In medicine, the *jing* (經) are the twelve meridians which run from the tips of the fingers to the tips of the toes. They are the movement from *yin* to *yang*, *yang* to *yin*; centre to periphery, and periphery to centre – the *yin* meeting in the area of the chest and the *yang* converging at the eyes. They create a continual cycle of regulation and maintenance, describing a north/south, heaven/earth axis, just like the meridians of the globe. The meridians of the body are spheres of influence, patterns of information transfer – the basis of the organization of the physical body. They connect with the five *zang* and six *fu*, creating *yin yang* relationships and describing the 'six divisions' of the body.

As the term *mai* includes all the various streams and tributaries, from the smallest to the largest – the *jing* are part of that circulation and provide the basic plan and pattern by which the whole system is controlled and regulated. Within the human body, the *jing* are the transmission of information to regulate the body in accordance with the natural order and with the source *qi*.

Suwen chapter 27:

> 'Heaven has its constellations, earth has its water courses (*jing shui* 經水), human beings have the *jing mai* (經脈)'.[165]

Lingshu chapter 12:

> 'The *jing mai* (經脈) are twelve. At the exterior they connect with the twelve water courses, at the interior they connect with the five *zang* and six *fu*. The five *zang* receive spirits and *qi* (*shen qi* 神氣) *hun* and *po* (魂魄) and store them; the six *fu* receive grains and circulate them, receive *qi* and spread them widely. The *jing mai* receive blood and provide sustenance (*ying* 營).'[166]

Whereas the *mai* are innumerable, there are only twelve *jing mai* (經脈) which are related to the internal organs in a *yin yang*, five phase coupling. It is on these twelve main meridians that the acupuncture points are located and where all treatment by acupuncture, massage, etc. takes place. (Two of the eight extraordinary meridians, the governor vessel, *du mai* 督脈, and conception vessel, *ren mai* 任脈, also have points, which we will see in the context of the extraordinary meridians). The twelve main channels have an interior/exterior, *yin*/*yang* relationship according to their five element pairings, but they are also distinguished into three types of *yin qi* – *shao yin* (少陰, lesser *yin*), *tai yin* (太陰 greater *yin*) and *jue yin* (厥陰 extreme *yin*), and three types of *yang qi*, *tai yang* (太陽, greater *yang*) *shao yang* (少陽, lesser *yang*) and *yang ming* (陽明 bright *yang*) creating

---

165 Lecture notes; Jing Luo
166 ibid.

pairings of *yin* with *yin* and *yang* with *yang*, which make up the *liu he* (六合), the six divisions or junctions.

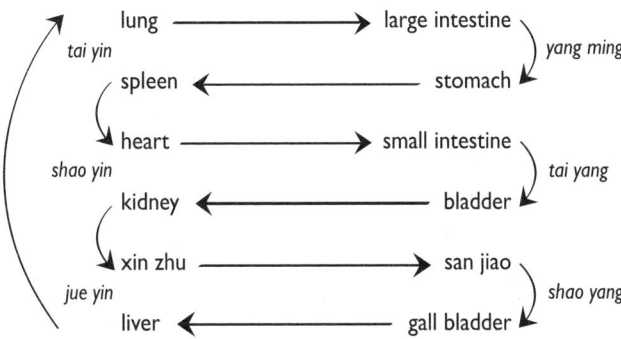

Fig. 13: meridian circulation

Meridian circulation is clearly described in Nanjing difficulty 23:

> 'The *jing mai* circulate blood and *qi*. They ensure the free communication of *yin* and *yang* so that the body can flourish. They begin in the middle heater, flow into the *tai yin* of the hand (lung meridian) and the *yang ming* of hand (large intestine meridian). The *yang ming* flows into the *yang ming* of the foot and the *tai yin* of the foot (stomach and spleen meridians). *Tai yin* flows into the *shao yin* and *tai yang* of the hand (heart and small intestine meridians); the *tai yang* flows into the *tai yang* and *shao yin* of the foot (bladder and kidney meridians). The *shao yin* of the foot flows into the *xin zhu* and *shao yang* of the hand (heart master/pericardium and triple heater meridians). *Shao yang* of the hand flows into the *shao yang* and *jue yin*

of the foot (gallbladder and liver meridians). The *jue yin* returns to flow once again into the *tai yin* of the hand (lung meridian).'[167]

Luo 絡

If the *jing* (經) are the weft of the weaving loom, the *luo* (絡) are more like the warp. The character has the silk thread radical and a phonetic (各) which has the meaning of variety – diffuse and different. Put together, *luo* (絡) is a network, or a series of threads making padding or wadding. It is also used with the meaning of to bind, or the binding around something.

We have seen the character *luo* in the term *xin bao luo* (心 包 絡), the protections and connections of the heart, where *luo* both reinforces the meaning of *bao* (包), the protective envelopment, but also suggests connectivity, a network which both protects and connects. The great *luo* of the spleen is unique in that it spreads out transversally across the trunk, enveloping the internal organs. As trajectories of the main meridians the *luo* reinforce the connections between *yin* and *yang*, interior and exterior, by passing between the *yin* and *yang* coupled channels and connecting via the *luo* points to the internal organs.

The term *luo* is also used to describe all the tiny vessels and capillaries flowing through the flesh, up to the surface and into the depths of the internal organs. There is no sense here of directional flow, but as suggested by the wadding or padding of the *luo* character, they bring circulation and connectivity into every part of the body. Lingshu chapter 10:

'The *jing mai* (經 脈), which are twelve, are buried in the depths

---

167 ibid.

where they circulate (*xing* 行) in the divisions (*bie* 別) of the flesh; being deep, one cannot see them. The *mai* which show on the surface are the *luo mai* (絡脈).'[168]

Jing bie 經別

The character *bie* (別) is used in the above text with the meaning of division and differentiation. It may also be translated as to diverge, and the *jing bie* (經別) are often called the meridian divergences. A *bie* is any kind of branching from the main meridian, but it is dependent on that meridian. In some texts the *luo* are said to detach (*bie*) from the main meridians, so there can be some confusion between the two terms. But the *jing bie* are quite specific, and the descriptions of their pathways are well documented in Lingshu chapter 11.

The *yin* channel divergencies generally link with the main meridian of their *yang* element partner, in order to ascend; the spleen, lung and kidney *jing bie* rise to the throat; the heart to the inner canthus of the eye and the pericardium to the ear. The liver *jing bie*, however, simply rises to the area of the perineum.

The *yang* divergencies tend to pass through both their associated organ and their *yin* element partner organ, but they link back with their own *yang* main meridian. The bladder divergent channel, for example, passes through the bladder and the kidneys, but it also contacts the anus and the base of the spine; it diffuses in the area of the heart before ascending to the back of the neck where it re-unites with the bladder main meridian.

---

168 ibid.

Jing jin 經筋

Jin is muscular strength, and the *jing jin* (經筋) act at the surface of the body but have a centripetal action. The character *jin* (筋) is made from the flesh (肉 contracted to 月), force or power (力) and the radical for bamboo (竹) at the top. The bamboo radical is used to represent all plant or fibrous growth, and its use here is a reflection of the structure of the muscles. The pathway descriptions suggest a kind of knotting or binding at the joints and a spreading into the bulk of the flesh. These knots or nodes are called the *jie* (節), which are stages of growth, often illustrated by the structure of bamboo, which has a knotting and gathering together before each new spurt of growth. These concentrations of the *jin jing* are effective places to treat injury. The character *jie* is used for many kinds of rhythmical or cyclical growth or progression, as we have seen, for example, in the nodes (*jie* 節) of the year.

Each of the twelve meridians is assigned a *jing jin*, which roughly, though with some interesting exceptions, follows the pathway of the main meridian. They bring blood and *qi* to the muscles and flesh, and maintain the function of the *wei qi* at the surface of the body.

The excellent Manual of Acupuncture[169] by Peter Deadman and Marzin Al Khafaji with Kevin Baker provides details of the pathways and functions of these various channels.

In the Nanjing, several chapters describe the *jing mai* as 'connected with the source of the vital *qi*'. For example, in Nanjing difficulty 8:

---

169 A Manual of Acupuncture, JCM Publications, 2005

'The twelve meridians, *jing mai* (經 脈) are connected to the source (*yuan* 原) of the vital *qi*. The source of the vital *qi* is the root and foundation of the twelve meridians, that is, 'the *qi* that moves between the kidneys' (*shen jian dong qi* 腎 間 動 氣). This is the foundation of the five *zang* and six *fu*, the root of the twelve meridians (*jing* 經) the gate of exhalation and inhalation; the source of the triple heater.'[170]

And similarly in Nanjing difficulty 66:

'The *qi* moving between the kidneys, below the navel, is the life destiny of a human being (*ren zhi sheng ming* 人 之 生 命), the root and foundation of the twelve meridians (*jing mai* 經 脈).'[171]

Here there is the suggestion that the twelve *jing mai* carry the information for the unfolding of life (*sheng ming* 生 命) and its continual rebuilding. The '*qi* that moves between the kidneys' is another way to describe this area within the belly – also variously called *ming men, bao zhong, dan tian* – from which life proceeds and is constantly renewed. This close connection with the original *qi* is seen clearly in the eight extraordinary meridians (*qi jing ba mai* 奇 經 八 脈), which act as a kind of intermediary between the origin and the differentiation of the twelve main channels. They are covered in detail in the next section as their classical origins are not discussed fully in most texts on the meridian system.

---

170 Heart Master Triple Heater, p. 106
171 ibid. p. 113

THE EIGHT EXTRAORDINARY MERIDIANS

Nanjing difficulty 27:

'The *mai* include the *qi jing ba mai* (奇 經 八 脈), eight *mai* which are not contained within the twelve meridians (*jing* 經).'[172]

The term *qi jing ba mai*, generally translated as the eight extraordinary meridians or vessels, contains both the characters *jing* and *mai* – and while they give the regulation suggested with the term *jing*, they do not adhere to the structure of the *wu xing/yin yang* coupling typical of the twelve main meridians. They therefore have an extraordinary (*qi* 奇) regulation (*jing* 經). This character *qi* is literally an exclamation of surprise, and is used to describe something wonderful, unusual, extraordinary. But it is also something that goes against the norm – and in classical Chinese

---

172 The Eight Extraordinary Meridians, Monkey Press 1997, p. 8

the character *qi* (奇) is often contrasted with the character *zheng* (正) which is to be correct and upright and to obey the rules. The twelve main meridians are described as *zheng*, and the *qi jing ba mai* are contrasted with them as being out of the ordinary, not following the usual rules. *Qi* (奇) may also be used to represent that which is left over – the remainder of a sum. For example, it is used to describe the adjustment of the rhythm of the year by adding an extra day to the calendar when necessary. It gives room for adjustment within a system that is man-made, to allow for the unpredictability of nature.

The remaining character is *ba* (八), eight, which is a significant number for the organization of space. In ancient times the eight winds were said to fill the eight points of the compass which represented all space. They were represented by the eight trigrams which structured and defined the intermingling of *yin* and *yang*.

So here are eight channels, which are outside of the ordinary patterning of the twelve regular (*zheng* 正) meridians, and which have an extraordinary function. We see in the Survey of Traditional Chinese Medicine that these channels '…represent the first organized circuitry of the energetic field'.[173] They are considered to be earlier in origin, and therefore closer to the source *qi*, and many commentaries suggest a relationship with development within the embryo, and therefore the prenatal *qi*. Postnatally, as the *zang fu* begin to function independently of the mother, the organization is made more specific by the twelve main meridians and their various divergent networks. With the first breath and the first ingestion of food, the embryonic organization of the eight becomes the more fully functional, independent twelve. But the *qi jing ba mai* continue to function throughout development and during adult

---

173 Survey of Traditional Chinese Medicine, p. 144

life ensuring a connection with the original patterning, and acting as a kind of intermediary between the twelve main meridians and their origin in the '*qi* that moves between the kidneys'.

The eight are not mentioned as a complete group within the text of the Neijing – and it is not until the Nanjing that the term *qi jing ba mai* is used – but each of the eight channels with their pathways and pathologies is discussed. Suwen chapter 60 is the source of the most detailed information on the extraordinary meridians, the texts of the Nanjing providing explanation and commentary on this seminal text.

We will look at each of the eight extraordinary meridians in turn, attempting to understand their function by looking at both the meaning of their names and also the descriptions of their pathways and functions in both the Neijing and the Nanjing. Only two of the eight, the *du* and *ren mai,* governor and conception vessels, have their own acupuncture points. The others share points with the ordinary meridians – these areas of exchange and interchange providing valuable information concerning their function and interrelationships.

DU MAI

Du mai (督 脈) is usually translated as the governor vessel. The upper part of the character (叔) has the meaning of uncle, usually the father's younger brother, and is used as a respectful way to address various male family members or friends with a close family association. It suggests someone who is close, responsible and trusted. One of the interesting associations with this phonetic is that together with the cloth radical (裘) it refers to the seam which runs down the back of a garment, just as the *du mai* follows the midline of the back. This character came to be used in the context of 'keeping in line with the centre'.[174] The lower part of the character is *mu* (目) the eye, or to see. *Du* (督) is the term used for an official, ruling an area on behalf of the emperor, possibly at the periphery of the empire and maintaining the security of the border. Traditionally, the post would have been held by a member of the emperor's family, someone trusted to look out for the emperor – a governor, or more literally a viceroy.

The *du mai* governs the *yang*. Running up the centre of the spine, it controls the *yang* areas of the back and the head, and the *yang* function within the *zang fu*. In Nanjing difficulty 28, which gives a short but definitive description of the pathways of the *qi jing ba mai*, it says of the *du mai*:

> '*Du mai* rises from the *yu* (俞) of the lower ridgepole (*xia ji* 下 極), it doubles the spinal column on the inside (*li* 裡); it rises up to *feng fu* (風 府, Du 16) and penetrates the brain with which it takes a belonging relationship.'[175]

Suwen chapter 60, on which this Nanjing difficulty is based, presents a very complex description of the pathway of *du mai*, suggesting that its influence covers much of the body, but here the text is simplified to its essence – the association with the spine, and with *feng fu* (Du 16), the

---

174 The Eight Extraordinary Meridians, p. 24
175 ibid. p. 27

acupuncture point at the base of the skull which has a direct connection to the brain. This emphasizes the function of *du mai* to ascend the clear *yang* to the brain, to bring clarity and enlightenment to the thinking, to the upper orifices, and to the perception. The 'belonging relationship' between *du mai* and the brain is the same as that which each of the twelve main meridians makes with its associated organ. Being the governor of the *yang*, the *du mai* also warms and moves the *qi*, ensures circulation, interpenetration and transformation.

Its pathway begins in the depths of the belly (*bao zhong* 包 中) and flows downwards to the perineum, where it surfaces. It then turns and rises up the spine, penetrating the brain, and continuing over the top of the head, it descends to the mouth. As it rises, it passes through the area of *ming men* (命 門) – which is also called 'the *qi* that moves between the kidneys'. We have already looked at the concept of *ming men*, the gate of life, and *ming men huo* (命 門 火), the fire in the lower belly. The acupuncture point *ming men* (Du 4) is located on this primary *yang* channel, on the spine at the level of the kidneys. The actions and locations of both *ming men* and *feng fu* illustrate the functions of *du mai*: its connection with the origin or gate of life; its ability to warm and move through the original fire of *ming men*; the clarification and purification of *qi* as it passes through the gates and doors of the *du mai* until it reaches the brain.

Many daoist and other yogic practices refer to a refining process which takes place within the subtle energy channels in the spine, and *du mai* is activated through breathing practices, visualizations or simply by paying attention. We now have so much more information about the functioning of the spinal nerves, and their relationship with the internal organs – and can appreciate this central position given to *du mai* for both the normal functioning of the human body, and also any attempt to refine and enhance its function. This was all well understood by the ancient Chinese, and the *du mai* is seen as the primary channel for the functioning of life.

REN MAI

The character *ren* (任) is made with the radical of the human being (人) and the phonetic *ren* (壬), which Wieger's Chinese Characters suggests is a representation of a bamboo pole carrying a load at either end[176], a very typical way of carrying things in East Asia until recent times. It has the meaning to bear a load, to endure something – and with the character for woman as radical (妊) it means to be pregnant. This is possibly the origin of the translation as conception vessel, but while the ability to conceive is certainly related to the *ren mai*, its influence is much wider in scope. With the radical of the silk thread (紝), the character means to weave, and this reflects the basic relationship between the *yin* and the *yang* – *yang* providing the guidelines and overseeing the development, *yin* providing the sustenanace and form. *Yin* weaves the physical structure onto the guiding *yang* threads.

    Ren (任) means to take up a position of responsibility, to undertake a task, to bear and to endure. The *ren mai* has the *yin* responsibility to protect and to nurture, which is of course the basis of the ability to carry a

---

176 Wieger's Chinese Characters, Lesson 82 C

foetus to maturity. But as well as the ability to both produce and nourish a child, the *ren mai* is that inner capacity of each individual to continually nourish and maintain life. It ensures production and reproduction – of another being, but also of ourselves. It envelops and protects, nourishes and maintains, and is therefore of great importance in providing the right environment for the protection and development of the child within the womb.

As the *du mai* is the original *yang* channel, so the *ren mai* is the original *yin* channel. And as *du mai* governs the back, *ren mai* governs the front, its pathway following the front midline. It arises in the *bao zhong* (包中), some commentaries suggesting that *du mai* and *ren mai* share this common origin and separate at the perineum.

Nanjing difficulty 28:

> '*Ren mai* arises below the middle summit, *zhong ji* (中 極 Ren 3), rises to the border of the (pubic) hair; it passes along the abdomen on the inside; it rises to *guan yuan* (關 元 Ren 4); it reaches the throat, larynx and pharynx (*hou yan* 喉 咽).'[177]

From this common pooling in the perineum, *ren mai* turns and ascends to the pubic bone, and rises to *zhong ji* (中 極 Ren 3) the middle summit, where it binds with the three *yin* channels of the legs (kidneys, spleen and liver), and on to *guan yuan* (關 元, the passage to the origin, Ren 4). As Du 16, with its pathway to the brain, expresses a key function of *du mai*, so Ren 4, the passage to the origin, expresses a key function of *ren mai*.

---

177 The Eight Extraordinary Meridians, p. 88

Guan yuan is usually translated as 'gateway to the origin', but it is a different kind of gateway to that implied in *ming men*. Both Ren 4 (*guan yuan* 關 元) and Du 4 (*ming men* 命 門) connect to the origin via a gate, but *men* (門) is a large open gate, which allows free access; *guan* (關) suggests that a key or a password, or some device is needed to gain entry. This passageway to the origin is protected and hidden, and provides a connection to the womb, and the hidden centre of life. As an acupuncture point, Ren 4 is important for treating the *yin* and the blood, and it has a connection with the uterus. *Ren mai* builds and nourishes life with blood and fluids.

From *guan yuan*, the *ren mai* ascends, passing through the sea of *qi* (*qi hai* 氣 海, Ren 6), spirit watchtower (*shen que* 神 闕, Ren 8) at the navel, rising to the central palace of the chest (*tan zhong* 膻 中, Ren 17), the upper sea of *qi*, before diffusing into the throat. Other texts describe the *ren mai* as ascending the throat and binding around the mouth, with a trajectory to the eyes. Suwen chapter 60, for example, begins in the exact same way as the Nanjing text, but adds:

> '…it rises to the chin, passes through the face and penetrates the eye.'[178]

The *ren mai* makes a complete circuit with the *du mai*, binding at the perineum, around the sexual organs, and also binding around the mouth. The *yin yang* polarity created between the *ren mai* and *du mai* deveops a kind of force field, which holds a dynamic potential, a potential which sparks the great *chong mai*, which spirals between them, uniting *yin* and *yang*, blood and *qi*, and providing a link between pre- and post-heaven.

---

178 ibid. p. 91

CHONG MAI

The *chong mai* (衝 脈) appears in third position in both Nanjing difficulty 28 and Suwen chapter 60. Often translated as the penetrating vessel, the character *chong* (衝) suggests a great force, a surging or rushing. The radical (行) is to move, to go – the *xing* of the *wu xing* – but is divided by the phonetic (重) which is an accumulation, a piling up. *Chong* (衝) is therefore a surging forward of something that has been accumulated. It is fast and strong. The character is also used to describe a main road or thoroughfare.

Nanjing difficulty 28:

> '*Chong mai* surfaces at *qi chong* 氣 衝 (St 30, the surging of *qi*, or *qi* thoroughfare); it doubles the pathway of the *yang ming* of the foot (the stomach meridian); it surrounds the navel and rises. It reaches the middle of the thorax (*xiong zhong* 胸 中) and diffuses there.'[179]

With its origin with *ren* and *du mai* in the lower abdomen, *chong mai* surfaces at *qi chong*, the great surging of *qi* on the stomach meridian at the level of the inguinal groove. In the Nanjing it is said to follow the stomach channel and diffuse into the chest. But we read in Suwen chapter 60:

---

179 ibid. p. 110

'*Chong mai* arises at the street of *qi* (*qi jie* 氣 街) St 30; doubling the pathway of the *shao yin* (the kidney meridian) it surrounds the navel and rises; it reaches the middle of the thorax (*xiong zhong* 胸 中) and diffuses there.'[180]

Both the name of St 30, here *qi jie* (氣 街), and the pathway of the meridian differ in this earlier text. There is another interesting description in Lingshu chapter 65:

'*Chong mai* and *ren mai* both arise in the middle of the intimate envelopes (*bao zhong* 胞 中); they rise, running up the back on the inside and make the sea of the *jing luo* (經 絡). Their pathway emerges and runs along the abdomen by the right and rises. They meet together at the pharynx; a divergence (*bie* 別) takes a *luo* (絡) relation with the lips and the mouth.'[181]

The *chong mai* emerges in the depths of the belly with the *ren mai* and *du mai*. The term *bao zhong*, translated literally here as the 'intimate envelopes' has been described elsewhere as 'gestational membranes',[182] an interesting translation which suggests a connection with the origins of life. It descends to the perineum and then surges upwards with a great force – a super-highway of *qi* – sometimes described as following the stomach channel and sometimes the kidney channel, and maybe uniting the prenatal *qi* of the kidneys with the postnatal *qi* of the stomach. From the lower abdomen the *chong mai* rises and diffuses into the chest. It links

---

180 ibid. p. 110

181 ibid. p. 116

182 Chase and Shima's Exposition on the Eight Extraordinary Vessels, 2010

the sea of *qi* in the abdomen (*qi hai* 氣 海) with the sea of *qi* in the chest (*tan zhong* 膻 中). The *chong mai* is known as the 'sea of blood',[183] the 'sea of the twelve meridians',[184] the 'sea of the five *zang* and the six *fu*'.[185] If *ren mai* and *du mai* are the expression of *yin yang* potential, *chong mai* is their coming together and realization.

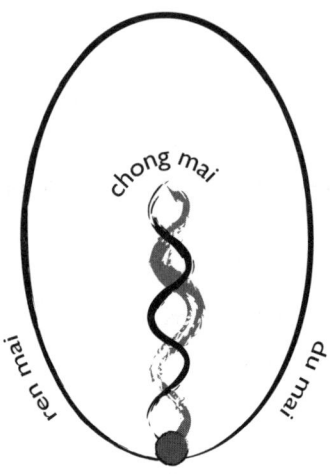

Fig. 14: the mutual arising of ren mai, du mai and chong mai

As the sea of blood, *chong mai* plays an important role in menstruation and fertility. Suwen chapter 1 discusses the cycles of fertility in men and women. We have already seen the important role of the kidneys, but for women, both the *ren* and *chong mai* play a vital role in fertility:

---

183 The Eight Extraordinary Meridians, p. 124
184 Lingshu chapter 62, ibid. p. 115
185 Lingshu chapter 38, ibid. p. 112

> 'At two times seven years, fertility (*tian gui* 天 癸) arrives; *ren mai* (任 脈) functions fully and the great *chong mai* (太 衝 脈, *tai chong mai*) rises in power (*sheng* 生); the menses flow downwards in their time and she is able to have children…'

> 'At seven times seven years, the *ren mai* is empty, the *tai chong mai* declines progressively, fertility dries up. Nothing passes through the way of earth (*di dao* 地 道); the body declines, and she no longer has children.'[186]

It is the combination of the *yin* holding and nourishing power of *ren mai*, and the dynamic moving force of *chong mai* that regulates the menstruation. The *yin* power of *ren mai* holds and nurtures the child in the womb, while the force of *chong mai* enables birth. These two together combine to enable the body of a woman to conceive, to maintain a pregnancy and to give birth.

Other passages on the *chong mai* describe a pathway surging from *qi chong* (St 30) and flowing into the legs, pushing down, following, or possibly forging the pathway of the kidney meridian, to emerge at the sole of the foot.

Lingshu chapter 62:

> 'The *chong mai* is the sea of the twelve meridians (*jing* 經). With the great *luo* of the *shao yin* (kidney meridian), it arises under the kidneys and surfaces at the street of *qi* (*qi jie* St. 30). It runs along the upper part of the internal aspect of the thigh and obliquely penetrates the

---

186 The Way of Heaven, p. 69, 75

middle of the popliteal crease; it runs along the leg on the inside, together with the meridian of *shao yin*; it descends and penetrates behind the internal malleolus; it penetrates underneath the foot.'[187]

Because of this pathway into the legs and feet, *chong mai* clinically has a relationship with all kinds of flaccidity, weakness and even paralysis of the lower limbs.

DAI MAI

The fourth channel is the *dai mai* (帶 脈), and it completes the first circuitry of the *qi jing ba mai*:

'*Chong mai*, *ren mai*, *du mai* and *dai mai* form the first embryological structure, or the first generation of the extraordinary meridians.'[188]

The description of *dai mai* in Nanjing difficulty 28 is very simple:

'*Dai mai* arises from the last ribs; it turns once around the body.'[189]

---

187 The Eight Extraordinary Meridians, p. 115
188 The Survey of Traditional Chinese Medicine, p. 145
189 The Eight Extraordinary Meridians, p. 136

Dai (帶) is a belt. The upper part of the character shows the folds of fabric held in place. The bottom part suggests something – usually seen as something of value and significance – hanging from the belt. The character is also used with the meaning of a kind of chaining, as in a mountain chain, something that is linked together to make a whole. The *dai mai* is the only channel to bind around the body. Other *luo* channels have a transversal aspect, but *dai mai* binds around the body, some old illustrations suggesting that this may be a few times.

The texts speak of a relationship to the area of the *du mai* at the level of the kidneys,[190] a forward movement to the end of the ribs at Liver 13, sloping obliquely into the abdomen, following the gallbladder meridian through the point *dai mai* (帶 脈 Gb 26) to the area of *guan yuan* (關 元 Ren 4). The texts do not state directly that *dai mai* makes a connection between *ming men* (命 門 Du 4) on the back and *guan yuan* on the front of the body, but this is implied by some commentators. *Dai mai* is not a simple line drawn on the surface of the body, but more like a complete cross-section through the belly. It is described as holding the meridians in place like a binding around a bunch of sticks – too loose and they will fall out, go this way and that, too tight and they might break. *Dai mai* maintains the correct circulation within the meridians by subtly adjusting its tension. If *dai mai* is too tight, there will be constriction, lack of circulation; too little tension and the muscles may be weak, there may be prolapses, or a kind of leaking and seeping away of fluids and essences – a pathology known in Chinese medicine as *dai xia* (帶 下), *xia* being to go down, to descend.

'*Dai mai* takes all the *mai* under its command by linking them; it

---

190 Lingshu chapter 11 in The Eight Extraordinary Meridians, p. 137

ensures there is no erratic circulation. It is like tying a belt together which hangs down at the front.'[191]

The *dai mai* holds the meridians in place and ensures their ascending and descending movements. After the *yin yang* circuitry of the *du* and *ren*, and the central spiralling of the *chong*, *dai mai* provides a lateral boundary, while giving volume and solidity. It has a strong relationship with the musculature, and with the *zong jin* (宗筋 ancestral muscle) in the perineum. This ability to hold things in their proper place and to ensure the correct circulation relates also to carrying the child within the womb, giving birth, regulating menstruation, and in the male to the ability to sustain an erection. The seepage and leakages of *dai xia* (帶下) include all kinds of seminal emissions and vaginal discharges. And as with all the extraordinary meridians, but particularly with the first four, *dai mai* has an important part to play in fertility.

The *dai mai* is mentioned in relation to the *zong jin* in Suwen chapter 44, a key source of information concerning *wei* (痿) wilting or flaccidity syndrome. We have come across the term *wei* before in relation to the power of the kidneys to contain the *yin* and to nourish the muscles – the result of too little storage in winter leading to flaccidity (*wei* 痿) in the spring. *Wei* may be translated as impotence, depending on the context, but also implies a lack of circulation, possibly leading to paralysis, in the lower limbs. An interesting section of Suwen 44 links *chong mai* (through St 30, *qi jie* 氣街), *du mai* and *dai mai* in this particular pathology:

> '*Yin* and *yang* meet together at the ancestral muscle (*zong jin* 宗筋); they meet at the street of *qi* (*qi jie* 氣街, St 30)… all this

---

[191] Li Shizhen, quoted in The Extraordinary Meridians, p. 141

maintains a relation of dependence (*shu* 屬) with the *dai mai*, and one of connection (*luo* 絡) with the *du mai*. When the *yang ming* is empty, the *dai mai* no longer guides (*yin* 引); there is impotence (*wei* 痿), and the lower limbs no longer function.'[192]

The first four of the extraordinary meridians have their beginning in the area of *bao zhong* (包 中), the 'gestational membranes' in the lower abdomen; they all have a connection with the perineum. They form circuits and bindings – *du*, *ren* and *chong* bind in the perineum and again in the mouth; *dai mai* connects them laterally, binding around the other three. They are the first separation of *yin* and *yang* (*du* and *ren*), the emergence of the life force between that potential (*chong*), gathered in and connected by the fourth (*dai*), which brings the limitation and also expansion of space represented by the four directions.

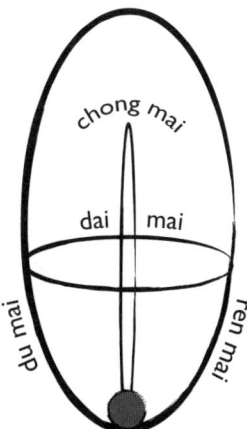

Fig. 15: the first four of the qi jing ba mai create frontal, dorsal, central and lateral extension

---

192 The Eight Extraordinary Meridians, p. 147

The second group of four extraordinary meridians comprises two *yin yang* pairs, *yin* and *yang qiao mai* (陰 陽 蹻 脈), and *yin* and *yang wei mai* (陰 陽 維 脈).

YIN AND YANG QIAO MAI

With this second group of channels we move from the concentration and origination within the trunk of the body to a surging up from the feet to the head. The character *qiao* (蹻) contains the radical for the foot (足) on the left; on the right, the phonetic (喬) has the original meaning of a high pavilion, and is used to describe something that is tall and erect. With the foot radical it means to stand erect, to be firm and stable, but also quick and agile. Commentators on the Nanjing suggest that the *qiao mai* give the ability to stand upright and walk. A common translation for the *qiao mai* is motility vessels.

Nanjing difficulty 28:

'*Yang qiao mai* (陽 蹻 脈) arises from the middle of the heel; it passes over the external malleolus and penetrates *feng chi* (風 池 Gb 20). *Yin qiao mai* (陰 蹻 脈) also arises from middle of the heel; it passes over the internal malleolus and rises; it reaches the pharynx where it crosses and then joins *chong mai*.'¹⁹³

These channels are bilateral; *yin* and *yang qiao* beginning together at the centre of both heels, separating and binding around the inner and outer malleolus respectively. At the heel and ankle, they assure mobility, flexibility and provide a firm rooting or anchoring before taking separate pathways, one on the *yin* aspect of the inner leg and the abdomen, the other on the outer, *yang* aspect of the leg and the back. In Nanjing difficulty 28, the *yang qiao* is associated with the point Gallbladder 20, (*feng chi* 風池), which reflects the association of *feng fu* (風 Du 16) with *du mai*; both points are at the nape of the neck and have a relationship with the brain. Wind (*feng* 風) appears in both point names, and this area of the nape of the neck is often associated with attack by external climates and is therefore in need of protection. But wind is also closely connected with the *yang qi* and the spirits, and as we have seen, Du16 is the gate where the pure *yang* is able to penetrate the brain. This is also suggested for Gb 20.

Other texts describe the meeting between *yin* and *yang qiao* at the eyes, as in Lingshu chapter 17:

> '…(*yin qiao mai*) enters below the eyes and has a communication with the inner corner of the eye, where it meets with the *tai yang* (bladder channel) and the *yang qiao*, and continues to rise.'¹⁹⁴

Meeting at the inner canthus, the *yin* and *yang qiao* adjust the opening and closing of the eyes, and their most frequently discussed classical

---

193 ibid. p. 163
194 ibid. p. 179

pathology is of insomnia and somnolence. They govern daily cycles of *qi* establishing rhythms for day and night. The text of Lingshu 21 quoted above continues:

'…When the *yang* are increasing in power the eyes are able to open; when the *yin* are increasing in power the eyes are able to close.'[195]

Lingshu chapter 21 describes the bladder channel having a relationship with the *qiao mai* at the eyes where there is also a penetration into the brain:

'…the pathways enters the brain and there is a separation of *yin* and *yang qiao*. This meeting and exchange takes place at the inner corner of the eyes.'[196]

The *yin* and *yang qiao* therefore make a complete circuit, having a combined origin at the heels and a gathering together at the eyes. In this they reflect the circuit of the *ren* and *du mai*. In certain daoist practices, the *ren* and *du mai* circuit is called the inner circulation, the *yin* and *yang qiao* the outer circulation. The technique of 'breathing through the heels' is thought to refer to this outer circuit of *yin* and *yang* within the body.

The *qiao mai* balance the *yin* and *yang* areas of the body and also the left and the right. Their relationship with the heels and the eyes reflects their importance in guiding the movement of *qi* from the feet to the head, and the head to the feet.

The movement through the *yin* and *yang qiao* also reflects the movement of *wei qi* (衛 氣, defensive *qi*), which is at the surface

---

[195] ibid. p. 186

[196] ibid. p. 186

during the day and in the depths of the body at night. It is this rhythm of exchange between *yin* and *yang*, between the inner and the outer, ascending and the descending, that defines the movement and function of the *yin* and *yang qiao mai*. Whereas *ren* and *du mai* balance *yin* and *yang* at a primitive level of functioning, remaining in contact with the origin of life, the *qiao mai* bring this balance into the rhythms and cycles of everyday life. The ability to stand up straight and walk; to balance, adjusting right and left; to sleep and replenish at night and wake and be active during the day – all these come under the influence and control of the *qiao mai*. In Lingshu chapter 17, Qi Bo likens their ebb and flow to 'the sun and the moon circling unceasingly'.

In certain texts the trajectories of the *qiao mai* are described as the *luo* (絡) of the kidney and bladder channels. Their points of detachment and anchoring are at Kidney 6 (*zhao hai* 照 海) and Bladder 62 (*shen mai* 申 脈), below the inner and outer malleolus respectively. These later came to be referred to as their 'master points', and are the main points for their treatment.

YIN AND YANG WEI MAI

Whereas cycles and alternation are the keynotes for the *yin* and *yang qiao*, the *yin* and *yang wei* are separate, with distinct functions and no interconnections. In Nanjing difficulty 28 they are not even described as having a pathway, but simply:

> '*Yang wei* (陽 維) and *yin wei* (陰 維) fasten and hold the body together (*wei luo* 維 絡)'.[197]

On the left, the character *wei* has the silk thread radical (糸). On the right the same phonetic (隹) that we saw in the *jiao* of *san jiao* (三 焦), triple heater, which has its etymological origins in a bird with a short tail, but came to represent a kind of layering and overlapping, as of feathers on a wing, forming a well constructed but pliable protection. With the silk thread, *wei* (維) has the meaning of holding and attaching, but also enveloping and protecting. A kind of gathering in.

Mythologically, the *si wei* (四 維) are the four attachments – the means by which all beings and things are suspended between heaven and earth. But the term was later used to define the four Confucian virtues which give the guidelines for mankind to live on the earth – civility, justice, integrity and truth; the four pillars of society. Many of the characters used to express principles and guidelines contain this idea of threads and nets – suggesting a thread of continuity, a lineage from heaven. Li Shizhen called the *wei mai* the *gang wei* (綱 維), *gang* being the great principle, but also the main rope of a net; that which holds things together. The *wei mai* sustain and maintain, while also providing a protective network to envelop and contain the physical structure. As we see in the Nanjing text, the *wei mai* 'fasten and hold the body together'. The term most commonly used in translation is the linking vessels. One commentary suggests:

---

197 ibid. p. 215

'That which is moving and circulating between all the *yang* meridians is called the *yang wei*; that which is moving and circulating between all the *yin* meridians is called the *yin wei*.'[198]

There is no concept of interchange between *yin* and *yang* as with the *qiao mai*. They do not meet or join. In the classical texts, they don't even have pathways as such. The *yang wei* is a function that maintains the *yang*, it limits at the exterior, protects and defends – it masters the *wei qi* (衛氣) and its presence at the peripheral parts of the body. The *yin wei* holds the *yin*, protects at the interior, and governs the *ying* (營) or nutritive *qi*. This is reflected in the pathologies mentioned in Nanjing difficulty 29, where an illness within *yin wei* affects the most inner aspect of the individual, the heart/mind, and therefore the spirits; an illness of the *yang wei*, the protection of the body from external climates:

'When the *yin wei* gives rise to illnesses one suffers from pain in the heart/mind. When the *yang wei* gives rise to illnesses, one suffers from cold and heat.'[199]

These attributes of the *yin* and *yang wei mai* are reflected in their master points, the gate to the interior, (*nei guan*, 內關 P 6) and the gate to the exterior (*wai guan* 外關, TH 5) respectively.

The *yin* and *yang wei* provide a network of connections, that bind and protect the *yin* and connect and diffuse the *yang*. *Yin* and *yang* are essentially a movement of *qi*, a movement towards the interior and towards the exterior, one always rooted within the other. This is also seen

---

198 ibid. p. 214
199 ibid. p. 225

in Nanjing difficulty 29:

> '*Yang wei* connects the *yang*, *yin wei* connects the *yin*. When *yin* and *yang* cannot connect with one another, there is vexation (*chang ran* 悵然) and loss of will (*zhi* 志). One is without strength, and no longer has hold of oneself.'[200]

This is a state of complete breakdown where *yin* and *yang* no longer communicate. It is not on the level of the rhythms and cycles and pathway interconnections of the *qiao mai*, but at a deeper level of the very innermost aspects of life not connecting with the outer; the nutritive and protective *yin* not relating to the defensive and transformative *yang*. The fire meridians of the *xin zhu* (heart master/pericardium) and *san jiao* (triple heater) in their *yin yang* relationship express this well. The *xin zhu* is the heart's ability to master the *zang* – and also the innermost aspects of the psyche, the spirits and emotions. The *san jiao* transforms the *qi*, diffusing the source *qi* right up to the surface of the body.

Li Zhongzi[201] describes the functions of the extraordinary meridians in this short passage:

> '*Du mai* has mastery of the *yang* at the rear of the body, and the *ren mai* of the *yin* at the front. *Dai mai* is like a horizontal link tying together all the vital circulation, and it corresponds to the six junctions, *liu he* (六合). *Yang wei mai* masters *biao* (表, exterior, movement towards exterior); *yin wei mai* masters *li* (理, interior or movement towards

---

200 ibid. p. 225
201 16th C contemporary of Li Shizhen

interior). *Yang qiao* has a special mastery of the *yang* on the left and right side of the body and the *yin qiao* a special mastery of the *yin* on the left and right side of the body in order to indicate their order and rhythm and inter-relationship.'[202]

Li Zhongzi does not mention the *chong mai* in his summary, and it has been suggested by many scholars that the *tai chong mai* (the great thoroughfare) is the source of all the extraordinary meridians, and the way in which original essence is distributed throughout the body. It is a term that is referred to extensively in alchemical texts.

Li Shizhen, author of the great 'Exposition on the Eight Extraordinary Vessels', considered the knowledge of these channels to be of primary importance for physicians, both for the practice of medicine and for their own inner cultivation. Li suggests that if the body is able to return to a state of stillness, the eight extraordinary meridians gather and circulate original essence and *qi*.[203]

As the *jing mai* are likened to a system of waterways, and the human body is seen as a landscape saturated with springs and wells, streams and pools, rivers and seas – the eight extraordinary meridians are the deep natural reservoirs which contain the purest water. These are not simply man-made drainage ditches and cisterns to collect runoff during times of excess rainfall – they are the deep well-springs of life which must be treated with care. An understanding of their nature and function is essential to the practice of Chinese medicine, and to the nourishment of life.

---

202 The Eight Extraordinary Meridians, p. 18
203 See Chace and Shima for a full translation and discussion of Li Shizhen's Exposition.

The eight extraordinary meridians and foetal development

In the Survey of Chinese Medicine it is maintained that:

'The eight extraordinary meridians must be re-integrated into the embryo and organo-genesis in order for their function to be fully understood.'[204]

It is suggested that these channels maintain a kind of template for the development of the foetus according to the coding within the male sperm and female ovum; the primal tension between *yin* and *yang, ren* and *du mai,* providing the primitive axis for its development and unfolding.

Precise correlations can only be speculation, but this is a rich area for possible study and reflection, especially now that it is becoming possible to observe the early stages of embryogenesis with more and more accuracy.

It has been determined that the exact place where the sperm penetrates the ovum is the initial trigger point for the segmentation and consequent multiplication of cells. The egg is defined by its north south poles which set up 'lines of force', generally referred to as 'meridians'. The line of force associated with the point of penetration becomes the median plane of subsequent symmetrical development.[205] The foetus develops by folding and re-folding along the median plane until a new impetus moves the process in a different direction. Most foetal abnormalities seem to take place at the stage when the final folding along the central mid-line forms the facial features, and the limbs emerge from the transient Wolffian

---

204 The Survey of Traditional Chinese Medicine, p. 144

205 This research conducted on frogs also discovered that the process of cellular multiplication could be instigated by using a prick to any point; the frog would develop normally, but would be sterile. See Mind and Nature, Gregory Bateson, for more details.

ridge.[206] This may suggest that this is a difficult and possibly evolutionary transition. The generation of life is seen to occur in two main patterns, bilateral symmetry and spiralling. The embryo first establishes its bilateral symmetry and then moves out into the spiral action that is seen within the limbs and also in the final positioning of the internal organs, as they migrate from their alignment along the median plane.

Ren mai and *du mai* establish the initial bilateral symmetry; they allow early development to proceed in accordance with the ancestral patterning, in a constant process of *yin* and *yang* enfoldment – the *yang* describing the impetus for each new stage of development, the *yin* its consolidation. *Chong mai* both holds the centre and pushes towards the development into the limb buds. *Dai mai* also comes into play with this final lateral consolidation of the trunk.

The *qiao mai* take part in the formation of this new extended axis as they push out with the heels from the centre to the extremities. From their joint rooting within the heels to their meeting at the eyes, they check left and right, rising and sinking, and maintain this balance as the individual develops its independent cycles of sleeping and waking, and eventually stands up and walks. Meanwhile the *wei mai* act independently from each other – the *yang wei* assuring the development of a good defence and immunity, the *yin wei* developing the inner possibility of nurture and alignment with the heart.

After birth, eight extraordinary meridians continue to function at a deep level, as a constant support system to the *jing mai* as the child grows and becomes an adult. They retain the link to the original patterning, and are considered in the treatment of any situation related to inherited

---

206 This structure develops within the embryo at around 4 weeks and encircles it laterally. The limb buds emerge from this temporary ridge. The migrating cells from the ridge are found in the genitals, mouth and nipples. At 4 weeks the embryo is 4mm long.

tendencies, early childhood patterns, and developmental issues. They are also widely used in the area of fertility. According to Elisabeth Rochat de la Vallée:

> 'Whenever the pattern of the 12 main meridians is unable to deal with the situations of life, it is possible to return to this deeper, more ancient system of regulation.'[207]

---

207 The Eight Extraordinary Meridians, p. 11

AFTERWORD

The sages and physicians of ancient China developed their philosophy through close observation of the world. They were not so much concerned with naming and classifying, but with understanding the way things work. They did not separate and look for building blocks, as did their contemporaries in Greece, but evolved a philosophy of connection and relatedness. They observed the movement of life, rather than its components. They were concerned with the way in which life emerges and the way that it returns – in a cyclical process of appearance and disappearance. They spoke of this as the mystery of life, the movement of the *dao*, the action of the spirits: but this was not simply philosophical speculation, they were engaged in the practical task of finding the best and most efficient way to live. Their concerns with spirits were never divorced from the need to eat and sleep, work and rest.

The early chapters of the Neijing Suwen, which have been the main focus of this book, embed medical theory within this philosophical milieu, and bring its insights to bear on the way that the body works and functions, the extraordinary detail of the observation reaching into the most subtle and obscure. The short and concise chapter 8 of the Suwen, The Secret Treatise of the Spiritual Orchid, which outlines the functions of the *zang fu*, ends with a few lines on the problem of approaching these deep mysteries of life, and our inadequacies in attempting to explore and describe them:

> 'The supreme *dao* is in the imperceptible, it is change and transformation without end! How can we possibly know its origin? When one searches anxiously for it, it simply disappears. How can we understand the essence of things? Such is the difficulty of the

real world. What can we possibly do? Countless appearances and disappearances, out of which come the finest threads; fine threads which multiply until eventually you can weigh and measure them. By the thousands and ten thousands they increase and multiply, through development and growth they form the human body, which is governed by its rules.'[208]

The text of Suwen 8 recalls the words of systems biologist Gregory Bateson:

'It is as if the stuff of which we are made were totally transparent and therefore imperceptible; and it is as if the only appearances of which we can be totally aware are the cracks and planes of fracture in that transparent matrix.'[209]

There is an assertion in both of these views that life takes place within the imperceptible and the transparent. And as the life sciences begin to approach these intimate processes of life, they have much in common with the language of Chinese medicine. The language of connection, networks and information patterning is alien to Western biomedicine, but it is a language which fits quite comfortably with systems theory, chaos and complexity. The new life sciences recognize what they call 'web-like patterns of organization' within living systems, which maintain the integrity of the whole while undergoing continual structural change. Life processes are described as circular rather than linear, the regulation of body temperature and blood chemistry as 'emerging' through the cyclical

---

208 The Secret Treatise of the Spiritual Orchid, p. 170

209 Bateson, Mind and Nature, Dutton, 1979

inter-relationships of body systems. They describe 'matrixes of messaging material'; mind as immanent within all matter – life as immanently self-healing.

At a time when the Chinese medicine is struggling to define its place in the modern world, and is tempted to discard the more wacky elements of its past, maybe we should instead be fully engaging with the strange and unexplainable, and examining it in the light of these new disciplines. What if the Chinese insistence on spirit is able to throw new light on the role of consciousness in healing? And what if the very precise descriptions of *qi* flow within the traditional texts are able to inform emerging disciplines such as psychoneuroimmunology? Maybe we will find that there is some residual cellular memory connecting tissues of similar origin as they migrate through the developing foetus that can explain some of the more obscure connections made within both meridian and *zang fu* theory.

With increasingly subtle tools available for exploration, and the fields of biochemistry and biophysics moving towards more and more subtle levels of knowledge, maybe we will come closer to understanding the more obscure aspects of our medicine. Not by rejecting what is 'spiritual' and reducing *qi* to a simple electrical stimulus within the connective tissues – but by being willing to fully engage with the question, 'What is life?' – without preconceptions and prejudices of a simplistically spiritual or narrowly scientific world view. Chinese medicine has never been a medicine of either/or, but of and/also; it exists at that exciting place where science and spirit meet.

It is by looking into the very mechanisms of life that the new sciences are returning to a holistic and self-organizing view of the world. And as there is a return to an understanding of patterns of relationship, and the emergence of self-organizing structures, there is a new reverence towards life, which is often best described in a more poetic than scientific language.

The language of the classical texts, with its insistence on spirits and its attempt to reach back into the source of things, is often poetic and sometimes indistinct – it needs to be grappled with. Translation alone is never enough. This is material that needs to be expanded, debated and engaged with; put to the test in our lives and in our practice.

Over the past two millennia, the Chinese medical literature has been predominantly populated by the commentary of practitioners and scholars on the Huangdi Neijing. The Monkey Press series, Chinese Medicine from the Classics, takes this tradition forward into the modern Western world. The text of the Neijing provides the basis for *zang fu* theory that informs all our practice, and the detailed and extremely subtle information on the meridian networks provides understanding that is often lacking within education today. This introduction to the underlying philosophy of our medicine can only be a beginner's guide, but my hope is that by introducing some of the basic ideas and terminology it will make the texts more accessible and inspire further study.

INDEX

INDEX

akabane test 95
alcohol 50, 126
ancestral muscle 76, 188
anger 52, 121, 122, 123, 125-129
archetypal patterns 5, 6, 115
asthma 78
autonomic nervous system 82, 156

back *shu* points 40, 98
Baihutong 152
bamboo 17, 43, 45, 80, 172, 179
bao zhong 胞中 60, 117, 118, 119, 120, 173, 178, 180, 183, 189
bian hua 變化, change and transformation 2, 96
bilateral symmetry 199
birds 56, 122
birth 44, 73, 91, 155, 185, 188, 199
bitter taste 55, 57, 69, 88
black 37, 39, 141
bladder 30, 42, 84, 85, 94, 98-101, 103, 118, 172
bladder meridian 110, 170, 171, 172, 191, 192, 193
Bladder 62 163
body hair 77, 78, 101
bones 34, 35, 112, 113, 115-116, 136, 156, 162
Book of Changes 9
Book of Documents 14
Book of Rites 49, 155
brain 35, 47, 49, 68, 71, 91, 92, 101, 112, 113-115
breasts 53
breath 19, 26, 27, 73, 79, 80, 81, 82, 104, 108, 141, 151, 156, 175

cang 臟, storage 29, 30, 39, 56, 84, 118, 150, 161
cang 蒼, azure green 49
cang 倉, storehouse 69
Celtic calendar 17
Chinese calendar 17, 65, 90
Chinese New Year 18
chuan 傳, transportation 30, 95, 96

chuan hua 傳化, transportation and transformation   85, 96
Chunqiu Fanlu   157
Chunqiu Zuozhuan, Spring and Autumn Annals   14
cold   7, 8, 9, 10, 16, 19, 25, 32, 33, 34, 37, 38, 76, 78, 91, 124, 161, 195
cold uterus   33
compass   4, 5, 175
Confucian virtues   126, 127, 138, 194
Confucianism   127, 157
consciousness   23, 56, 61, 71, 114, 145-151, 156, 203
cosmology   1, 16
coughing   79, 83
cou li 腠理   100, 101
cramps   46

dai xia 帶下   187, 188
dampness   19, 45, 66, 67
Daodejing   2, 167
Daoism   1, 146
daoist practices   113, 132, 192
death   6, 11, 79, 98, 141, 145, 151, 153, 155, 156
destiny   1, 22, 40, 108, 126, 161, 173
digestive system   45, 68
dreams   51, 52, 150, 151
Du 4, Ming men   187, 181, 187
Du 16, Feng fu   177, 180, 191
Du 20, Bai hui   114
du mai 督脈   40, 101, 168, 176-179, 180-189

ears   38, 58, 61, 83, 114,
eczema   78
eight   9, 175
eight year cycles   33, 36, 47, 93
elation   57, 63, 64, 121, 123, 124, 129-131, 161
embryo   24, 118, 119, 175, 198, 199
embryogenesis   198
energetic field   175
erection   46, 47, 128, 188
ethereal soul   51, 145
eyes   24, 37, 47, 50, 51, 61, 83, 127, 132, 167, 181, 191, 192, 199

fascia 110
fear 37, 38, 83, 121, 122, 123, 133-137, 143, 160
feng shui 風水 9
fertility 18, 19, 32, 33, 36, 41, 47, 159, 184, 185, 188, 200
festivals 18, 55, 129
five tastes 29, 58, 69, 70, 86, 88, 137
flaccidity 47, 186, 188
foetus 73, 109, 179, 198, 203
four gates 17
four images 9, 12
four limbs 70, 71, 89, 142
four seasons 8, 11, 13, 16, 27, 31, 65, 121, 137, 144, 160, 162
free-flow 44, 46, 51, 52, 53, 57, 76
Fuxi 5, 6

gao huang 高肓 109, 110
gestational membranes 183, 189
ghosts 18, 23, 79, 81, 153
grasp 48, 49, 50
Greek medicine 19
gui 鬼 22, 79, 81, 152, 156
Gun 15
Guo Yu 8, 15

hair 24, 36-37, 48, 77, 78, 79, 101, 113, 115, 180
Han dynasty 1, 13, 76
harvest 18, 19, 72, 75, 76
Heart 1, Ji quan 165
Heart 7, Shen men 60
hexagram 9, 41
Hongfan, Great Plan 14, 15, 17, 32, 35, 43, 54, 65, 75
Huainanzi 3, 4, 10, 109, 124
hun 魂 51, 52, 81, 84, 85, 145, 147, 148, 150-152, 153, 155, 161, 168

ileo-caecal valve 93, 95
imagination 51, 52
Imperial Palace 63, 64
impotence 47, 136, 188, 189
inguinal groove 182

intelligence   2, 56, 61, 81, 91, 93, 94, 97, 145, 156, 163
irritability   45, 53, 125, 126, 128
itching   45

jealousy   128
jin ye 津液   85, 87, 88, 99, 115
jing bie 經別   171
jing jin 經筋   171-172
jing wei 精味   26, 88, 105
jing wei 經痿, paralysis   114
judgement   76, 127, 132

Kidney 1, Yong quan   165
kuang 狂, madness   127, 132, 161

lan men 闌門   93, 95
late summer   19, 72, 76
laughter   57, 131, 132
Liji, Book of Rites   155
liquorice   68
Li Shizhen   114, 197
Liver 13, Zhang men   187
Li Zhongzi   196, 197
lower orifices   39, 46, 58
LSD   131
Lung 9, Tai yuan   81, 166
luo 絡   60, 61, 109, 118, 162, 164, 170, 185, 187, 189, 193, 194
Lüshi Chunqiu   6, 8
lymph   94

mai 脈, vital circulation   113, 116, 117, 150, 162, 164-166, 167, 168, 170, 174
malleolus   186, 190, 191, 193
Manual of Acupuncture   172
marrow   34, 35, 112, 113, 114, 115-116, 136
Mawangdui   60, 153
May Day   18
meditation   51, 150, 157
melancholic temperament   140
menstrual cycle   52, 53

ming 命 1, 22, 23, 24, 39, 161, 173
ming men 命 門 39, 40, 42, 49, 59, 81, 90, 100, 102, 106, 107, 109, 111, 117, 118, 119, 178, 181, 187
ming men huo 命 門 火 40, 107, 178
minister fire 58, 59, 61, 90, 108, 109,
moon 18, 152, 193
mouth 67, 68, 81, 178, 181, 183, 189, 199
muscular movement 45, 47, 50, 83, 162
mutual resonance 21, 97

nervous system 47, 62, 82, 101, 156, 163
Nugua 5, 6
nutrition 46, 74, 80, 89, 158
nutritive *qi* 70, 117, 195

oppression 57, 83, 121, 122, 123, 140-142, 158
Oschman, James 110
ovum 32, 198

paralysis 71, 114, 186, 188
pentatonic scale 37, 49
perineum 46, 47, 171, 178, 180, 181, 183, 188, 189
po men 魄 門 82, 95
post-heaven 73, 74, 89, 109, 181
postnatal *qi* 183
pregnancy 47, 95, 119, 185
pre-heaven 73, 74, 109
premenstrual tension 128
prenatal *qi* 175, 183
primal chaos 5
pulse 27, 56, 94, 100, 117, 164, 166
pungent 77, 78

qing su 清 肅, descending the clear 78

reflection, *lü* 盧 138, 144, 147, 148
Ren 4, Guan yuan 95, 180, 181, 187
Ren 6, Qi hai 181
Ren 8, Shen que 181

Ren 17, Tan zhong   181
reproduction   40, 180
rhythm   19, 27, 63, 82, 155, 166, 175, 193

sadness   79, 117, 121, 122, 123, 140-142
salty taste   34, 35, 57, 88
scales   75, 76, 142
sea of blood   113, 184
sea of five *zang* and six *fu*   88
sea of liquids and grains   87, 105, 114
sea of marrow   35, 113, 114, 115
sea of nourishment   87
sea of *qi*   27, 63, 82, 104, 113,
sea of the twelve meridians   184, 185
seizures   46
seven year cycles   32, 33, 36, 185
shaking   44, 46, 53, 133,
Shang dynasty   22
sheng 生 cycle   73
shiver   37
shout   49, 52, 130
Shuowen Jiezi   165
sighing   49, 83
sight   50, 51, 62
six junctions   162, 196
skin   27, 37, 77, 78, 79, 83, 83, 96, 97, 100, 101, 161
skull   177
sobbing   79, 83
sorrow   141, 142, 158
sour taste   45, 69, 78, 83, 88
sovereign fire   58, 59, 61, 62, 107
speech   58
spaced-out   57
spasms   46
sperm   24, 32, 33, 36, 41, 118, 198
spinal chord   46
spring   11, 12, 13, 17, 18, 33, 43, 44, 47, 49, 54, 55, 65, 77, 90, 160, 188
Spring and Autumn Annals   14
square   5

Stomach 25, Shen que 97
Stomach 30, Qi chong, Qi jie 87, 182, 183, 185, 188
Stomach 37, Ju xu xia lian 95, 97
Stomach 39, Ju xu shang lian 95
sun 7, 8, 19, 43, 54, 58, 64, 66, 67, 78, 193
Sun Simiao 111
sweet taste 66, 68, 69, 83, 88

Taisu 60
tai yi 太一, great unity 7
tan zhong 膻中 62, 63, 64, 104, 181, 184
teeth 36, 37, 48, 115
Temple of Heaven 63, 64
thought 67, 68, 83, 123, 137, 139, 145, 147, 148, 157, 159
tongue 58, 83
trembling 46, 53
true nature 1, 22, 23, 24, 122, 130, 136, 138, 145

uterus 33, 40, 41. 46, 52, 60, 95, 112, 113, 117-119, 181

visions 51, 52, 131
visualization 51
vital circulation, *mai* 脈 55, 56, 64, 87, 94, 112, 113, 116-117, 118, 166, 196

weapons 17, 75
wei 痿, flaccidity 47, 188, 189
wei qi 衛氣, defensive *qi* 27, 82, 89, 106, 108, 172, 192, 195
Wieger's Chinese Characters 165, 179
wisdom 137, 147, 148
Wolffian Ridge 198
womb 73, 180, 181, 185, 188
wu cai 五材, five substances 14
wu shen 五神, five aspects of spirit 51, 145, 148, 157
wu wei 五味, five tastes 26, 69
wu xing 無形, no form 6, 61, 108
wu xing 五行, five elements, phases, movements 13-21, 94, 121, 174, 182

xiang 象, pattern, image 4, 10, 12
Xici 23

xin bao luo 心包絡   60, 61, 63, 107, 109, 118, 170

yang ming 陽明   89, 92, 98, 168, 169, 182, 189
yang sheng 養生, nourishing life   147
yi 意, intent   71, 142, 145, 147, 149, 156-158, 159, 160, 161
Yijing, Book of Changes   9, 23, 40, 167
ying qi 營氣   *27,* 70, 82, 105, 108
you men 幽門   92
yun hua 運化   65
Yun men, Lung 2   78
yuan qi 原氣   26, 27, 32, 39, 73, 107, 108, 118

zao po 糟粕, residues and waste   96
Zhang Jiebin   103
Zhuangzi   151, 165
zi ran 自然   1
zong jin 宗筋   46, 47, 188
zong mai 宗脈   47
zong qi 宗氣   26-27, 46, 47, 63, 82, 104, 108

GLOSSARY of frequently used Chinese terms

ai 哀 grief, affliction

bao 包 to protect, to envelope, as in *xin bao luo* 心包絡, the protections and connections of the heart, and *bao zhong* 包中 protections of the centre of life in the belly
bao 胞 uterus or gestational membranes
bei 悲 sadness; emotion often related to the lung
bian hua 變化 change and transformation, the activity of the life processes
biao 表 the outer, movement towards the exterior
bie 別 divergence, *jing bie* 經別, channel divergence

cang 臧 to store, to treasure
cang 倉 storehouse, *cang lin* 倉廩, storehouses and granaries, function of the spleen and stomach
cang 蒼 azure green, the colour related to wood in Suwen 5
chuan hua 傳化 movement and transformation; the activity of the *fu* organs
cou li 腠理 the fine markings at the surface of the skin; the inter dermal layers of the skin

da chang 大腸 large intestine
dai xia 帶下 discharges, particularly vaginal discharges related to *dai mai* pathology
dan 膽 gallbladder
dan tian 丹田 literally, cinnabar field; the three areas of daoist alchemical transformation – the lower in the belly, the middle in the heart, the upper in the brain
dao 道 the movement of life
de 德 the expression of the movement of life within living beings
di 地 the earth, as coupled with heaven

fei 肺 the lungs
feng 風 wind

fu 腑 the *yang* organs of digestion and transportation; stomach, gallbladder, small intestine, large intestine, bladder, triple heater

gan 肝 the liver

gao huang 膏肓 primitive tissues found in the area of the heart and diaphragm, the navel and *ming men*

gui 鬼 the spirits of the earth, as contrasted with *shen*, the spirits of heaven

huo 火 fire

hun 魂 the aspect of the soul which leaves the body at death and travels in dreams and meditations; *yang* partner of the *po*

jiao 焦 heater, warming space; the *san jiao* 三焦 triple heater, or three warming spaces

jie 節 regulation, rhythm

jin 筋 muscular movement, muscular strength

jin 金 metal

jin ye 津液 bodily fluids; *jin* the more light, *ye* the more dense

jing 精 essence, the most subtle of material substance, inherited at birth and associated with kidneys

jing 經 meridian, the twelve main meridians; regulation; transmitted text, as in Neijing 內經

jing 驚 fright, jumpiness

kong 恐 fear, emotion associated with the kidneys and the water element

kuang 狂 madness

lan men 闌門 gate between small and large intestines

le 樂 joy, emotion associated with the heart and the fire element

li 裡/理 inner, movement towards the interior; the inner structure as it manifests itself at the exterior

liu he 六合 the six junctions; within the body, the six divisions of *qi* – *tai yang, yang ming, shao yang, tai yin, jue yin, shao yin*

lü 盧 reflection, concern

luo 絡   network of connection; lateral connection between channels; a network of small capillary-like vessels

mai 脈   vital circulation, circulation of *qi* and blood and its measurement at the pulse
ming 明   illumination, brilliance (joint illumination of sun 日 and moon 月), as in *shen ming* 神明, illumination of the spirits
ming 命   destiny, inherited life span, mandate of heaven
ming men 命門   gate of destiny, gate of life, where life is received and renewed; name of acupoint Du mai 4
mu 木   wood

nu 怒   a dynamic surge of *qi*, the upward thrust of the life-force; anger, the emotion associated with the liver and the wood element

pang guang 膀胱   the bladder
pi 脾   spleen
po 魄   the aspect of the soul which returns to the earth at death; the intelligent but unconscious organization of the body; *yin* partner of the *hun*
po 粕   waste; *po men* 粕門, anus

qi 氣   that which animates, transforms and maintains all life between heaven and earth
qi 奇   extraordinary, amazing
qi kuo 氣口   the opening of *qi*, the pulse
qing 情   emotion, inner disposition
qing 清   clear, pure

san jiao 三焦   triple heater, three burning spaces etc.; one of the six *fu*
shen 腎   kidneys
shen 神   spirits of heaven; consciousness
shen 身   the body
sheng 生   the generation of life; *yang sheng* 養生 nourishing the generation of life

shui 水 water

si 思 thought, obsessive thought, related to the spleen and the earth element

tai yuan 太淵 the great abyss, acupoint Lung 7; the place where the *qi* wells up in the radial artery and where the pulse is taken

tan zhong 膻中 the central palace in the chest; attributed one of the twelve charges in Suwen chapter 8; name of acupoint Ren 17

tian 天 heaven, the natural progression of things

tu 土 earth, soil; the earth element

wai 外 outer, external

wei 胃 stomach

wei 衛 defence, *wei qi* 衛氣 defensive *qi*

wei 痿 flaccidity, weakness, impotence; as in *wei* syndrome

wu shen 五神 the five aspects of spirit, mind and consciousness, *shen* 神, *hun* 魂, *po* 魄, *yi* 意 and *zhi* 志

wu cai 五材 the five elemental substances

wu xing 無形 no-form; the state before physical manifestation

wu xing 五行 five movements, phases, elements

xi 喜 elation; emotion related to the heart and to *tan zhong*

xiang 象 image, pattern; energetic formation before physical manifestation

xiao chang 小腸 small intestine

xin 心 heart

xin zhu 心主 heart in its mastering function

xing 性 true nature, generation of life through the heart

xing 行 regular movement, *wu xing* 五行 the five phases, five elements

xing 形 form

xue 血 blood

yang 陽 that which is warming, motivating and expansive

yi 意 intention, attention; aspect of spirit/consciousness associated in medicine with the spleen

yin 陰 that which is cold, contractive and conserving

ying 營 nutrition, construction, maintenance; *ying qi* 營氣 nutritive *qi*
you 憂 oppression, oppressive grief, emotion associated with the lungs and metal
yuan 原, 元 origin, source, *yuan qi*, original or source *qi*

zang 臟 the *yin* organs of storage; heart, kidneys, liver, spleen and lung
zao po 糟粕 residues and waste
zheng 正 regular, ordinary (often contrasted to *qi* 奇 extraordinary)
zhi 志 will; aspect of spirit/consciousness associated in medicine with the kidneys
zhi 知 wisdom; the practical wisdom to live efficiently
zhong 中 centre, central
zi ran 自然 that which is naturally so
zong 宗 ancestral, gathering; as in *zong qi* 宗氣 the gathering of *qi* in the chest; *zong mai* 宗脈, the gathering of the meridians around the eyes; *zong jin* 宗筋 the gathering of the musculature in the perineum

TEXT REFERENCES

These documents appear as references within the text. Translations of the Chinese have been made by Claude Larre and Elisabeth Rochat de la Vallée unless otherwise stated. Some recommended English translations of Chinese texts are included.

Baihutong: On the interpretation of the Classics, attributed to Ban Gu, 1st century CE. Qinghua Shuji, Beijing, 1994.

Chunqiu Fanlu: Attributed to Dong Zhongshu, 2nd century BCE; *yin yang* and *wu xing* theory. Several chapters, including Heaven, Earth and Yin Yang and The Meaning of the Five Elements, translated by Fung Yulan, 1934.

Chunqui Zuozhuan: Fourth century BCE commentary by Zuo on the Spring and Autumn Annals (particularly the history of the State of Lü between 722-468 BCE). English translation by James Legge.

Daodejing: The Classic of the Way and its Virtue. Otherwise known as the Laozi. Foundation text of Daoism probably from around 5th century BCE. Many translations available.

Guanzi Neiye: An eclectic text, with sources from 4th century BCE; it includes the chapter Neiye, Inward Training. Parts of the Guanzi have been translated by A.C. Graham in Disputers of the Dao (Open Court 1989); Original Dao is a study of the Neiye by Harold D. Roth (Columbia University Press, 1999).

Guo Yu: Discourses of the Kingdoms, a collection of historical accounts of the Zhou dynasty, collated around the 5th century BCE.

Hongfan: The Great Plan, a chapter of The Book of Documents (Shujing), one of the Five Classics, which records possibly mythical as well as early historical events from the Shang and Zhou dynasties. The Hongfan contains some of the earliest known references to *wu xing*, five phase/element theory.

Hua Tuo: Renowned physician from the 2nd century CE.

Huainanzi: Syncretic daoist text of the 2nd century BCE. Complete text translated and published in 2010 by Columbia University Press. Quotes are from Jing Shen, a group translation of chapter 7, Monkey Press, 2010. See also, *Yuan Dao: Tracing the Dao to its Source*. Roger Ames and D. C. Lao, Translation and commentary on Huainanzi chapter 1.

Li Shizhen: Physician of the 16th century, author of several texts including The Treatise on the Eight Extraordinary Meridians, translated by Charles Chase and Miki Shima. Eastland Press, 2010.

Lunyu: The Analects of Confucius. Probably collated in the 5th century BCE, though possibly a later Han dynasty revision of an earlier collection.

Lüshi Chunqiu: Spring and Autumn Annals of Lüshi, a compendium of knowledge compiled mid 3rd century BCE. English translation and commentary John Knoblock and Jeremy Riegel, Stanford University Press, 2000.

Manual of Acupuncture: Peter Deadman, Marzin Al-Khafaji with Kevin Baker, most comprehensive text in English on channels, collaterals, point location, point selection and needling. Journal of Chinese Medicine Publications, 2005

*Mawangdui Manuscript*s: Unearthed from the Mawangdui tombs in 1972; Medical manuscripts translated by Donald Harper as *Early Chinese Medical Literature*, Kegan Paul International; 1998

Mind and Nature, A Necessary Unity: Gregory Bateson; Dutton, New York, 1979

Nanjing, The Classic of Difficult Issues; attributed to Ban Gu, 1st century CE. English translation by Paul Unschuld; University of California Press, 1986.

Shuowen Jiezi: Explaining and Analysing Chinese Characters, Xu Shen, 121 CE. Translated and abridged as *Chinese Characters* by Dr L. Wieger, Dover Books, 1965.

Sun Simiao: Sui-Tang dynasty physician, author of Essential Formulas worth a Thousand Pieces of Gold, he also wrote several texts on *yang sheng* (nourishing life practices) and the treatment of women. Several of the works of Sun Simiao have been translated by Sabine Wilms and published by Paradigm Press.

Survey of Traditional Chinese Medicine: Claude Larre, Elisabeth Rochat de la Vallée, Jean Schatz, translated from the original French by Sarah Stang; Institut Ricci, Paris, Traditional Acupuncture Foundation, Maryland, 1986

Taisu: One of the great compilations of the medical texts (Sui Dynasty)

Xici: Commentary on the Book of Changes (Yijing)

Yijing (I Ching): The Book of Changes. One of the Five Classics; a book of divination, considered to predate written history. Traces are to be found on Shang and Zhou dynasty oracle bones. The current text possibly an accretion of Zhou dynasty divination methods.

Zhang Jiebin: One of the principal commentators on the Neijing in the late Ming Dynasty. Emphasizing going 'back to the root', he was influential in the systemization of acupuncture theory.

Zhenjiu Jiayijing, The Systematic Classic of Acupuncture and Moxibustion, 3rd century CE; attributed to Huangfu Mi. English translation, Shuozhong Yang and Charles Chase, Blue Poppy Press, 1994.

Zhuangzi (Chuang Tzu): Daoist philosophical text from 4th century BCE. Complete text translated by Burton Watson, Columbia University Press, 1968.